SO-BSI-705

THE GREAT Tween BUYING MACHINE

Capturing Your Share of the
Multibillion Dollar Tween Market

David L. Siegel

Timothy J. Coffey

Gregory Livingston

Dearborn™
Trade Publishing
A **Kaplan Professional** Company

HUMBER DISCARD
3199 Lakeshore Blvd. West
Toronto, ON M8V 1K8

This publication is designed to provide accurate and authoritative information in regard to the subject matter covered. It is sold with the understanding that the publisher is not engaged in rendering legal, accounting, or other professional service. If legal advice or other expert assistance is required, the services of a competent professional should be sought.

Vice President and Publisher: Cynthia A. Zigmund
Acquisitions Editor: Michael Cunningham
Senior Project Editor: Trey Thoelcke
Interior Design: Lucy Jenkins
Cover Design: Design Solutions
Typesetting: the dotted i

© 2004 by David L. Siegel, Timothy J. Coffey, Gregory Livingston

Published by Dearborn Trade Publishing, A Kaplan Professional Company

All rights reserved. The text of this publication, or any part thereof, may not be reproduced in any manner whatsoever without written permission from the publisher.

Printed in the United States of America

04   05   06   10   9   8   7   6   5   4   3   2   1

Library of Congress Cataloging-in-Publication Data

Siegel, David L.
    The great tween buying machine : capturing your share of the multibillion dollar tween market / David L. Siegel, Timothy J. Coffey, and Gregory Livingston.
       p.   cm.
    Originally published: Ithaca, N.Y.: Paramount Marketing Pub., 2001.
    Includes bibliographical references and index.
    ISBN 0-7931-8599-8—ISBN 0-7931-8599-8
    1. Child consumers.   2. Market segmentation.   I. Title: Capturing your share of the multibillion dollar tween market.   II. Coffey, Timothy J.
III. Livingston, Gregory.   IV. Title.
HF5415.32.S55 2004
658.8′0083′4—dc22

                    2003026591

Dearborn Trade books are available at special quantity discounts to use for sales promotions, employee premiums, or educational purposes. Please call our Special Sales Department to order or for more information at 800-245-2665, e-mail trade@dearborn.com, or write to Dearborn Trade Publishing, 30 South Wacker Drive, Suite 2500, Chicago, IL 60606-7481.

C o n t e n t s

Humber College Library

SPECIAL THANKS

We would like to thank the many clients with whom we have had the privilege of serving over the past years. We are also grateful for the wonderful experiences, challenges, and learning opportunities that helped us in crafting this book.

While many friends, peers, and associates kindly provided us with their thoughts and help, the following deserve extra-special mention:

- *C&R Research/KidzEyes.com.* Much of our newest, most complete data has been generously provided by C&R Research and its online panel, KidzEyes.com. Headquartered in Chicago, C&R Research is a full-service consumer and business-to-business market research firm. For over 20 years, its researchers have pioneered and enhanced new techniques for talking with children of all ages. KidzEyes.com is a COPPA-compliant online research panel of over 5,000 kids. (e-mail: robbinj@crresearch.com)
- *LearningWorks.* Donald Lay, Managing Director of Learning Works, together with his staff, provided us with much of our chapter on tween education. Learning Works is a full-service educational marketing firm specializing in developing and implementing customized curriculum materials. With over 20 years of hands-on experience in education and marketing, LearningWorks personnel have produced over 500 school-targeted and family-targeted programs. (e-mail: learningworks@prodigy.net)
- *Michael Phelan.* Michael Phelan is an independent consultant helping companies develop the kid, tween, and teen business segments. Michael has become a specialist in helping companies use grassroots marketing and sports and entertainment assets to drive their business, and, as such, he provided us with the "behind-the-scenes" facts and figures for Chapter 12, "Finding Tweens at the Grassroots Level." Michael was formerly the general manager for Reebok Kids where he was responsible for product development and marketing for a $300 million category, creating product tar-

geted for kids age 5 through age 13, and launching the highly successful Reebok Traxtar. (e-mail: MJPhelan@Mediaone.net)

- *Initiative Media.* A significant part of our discussions on various media as well as on tween influence was aided by information and guidance provided by Initiative Media. Initiative Media Worldwide is the world's leading media services company which operates 71 offices in 43 countries on 6 continents. Initiative Media Worldwide is a member of the Interpublic Group of Companies. (e-mail: cheri.gardiner@initiativemedia.com)

- *Tricia Leahy, Sports Illustrated for Kids.* To assess trends in tween activities, Tricia Leahy, Marketing Research Manager of *Sports Illustrated for Kids,* provided us with data and analysis from the many *Sports Illustrated for Kids* Omnibus studies that were conducted over the past ten years. Tricia has been working in the kids and teens market for nearly 11 years and holds an MS in Elementary Education.

We would also like to extend a special thanks to Melissa Booth and Robin Richie, without whose help this revised version of *The Great Tween Buying Machine* would have been much less complete and much less timely. Our final thanks go to our families, whose support of our endeavors in youth marketing allow us personal insight as well as understanding during those long weeks that seem to coincide with continuing growth and success.

As a youth-marketing specialist for more than 20 years, I have had the opportunity to see and hear many humorous, sometimes touching examples of tween influence. One of my all-time favorites occurred several years ago, while flying to speak at a New Orleans kid conference. When he learned about my upcoming speaking engagement, the passenger sitting next to me told me of a recent incident involving his 8-year-old daughter.

He told me that his little girl influenced him to do something that his doctor, his peers, his wife, and others could not do. She influenced him to quit smoking.

When I told him that I wasn't at all surprised at this feat, he insisted that I listen to how she did it. I am glad that I did.

He told me that, a month before, his daughter came to him while he was smoking a cigarette and said, "Daddy, please stop smoking cigarettes." He said, "Sure hon, one day." She then said, "Daddy, please stop smoking your cigarettes." He said, "Sure honey, soon." Then she said, "No, daddy, please stop smoking your cigarettes right now, because if you don't you may need a new heart . . . and if you have a new heart, you won't love me anymore." He quit!

The power of today's tweens to influence their parents to buy or to do just about anything, plus the significance of their own spending and actions have become something that few savvy businesses can easily ignore.

Recently much has been written about the power of today's kids and the important market segment they have become. However, too many of these writings and, unfortunately, too many marketers try to lump all kids together.

To think of kids in groups such as 2 to 11 year olds, 2 to 14 year olds, or, even worse, 2 to 16 year olds is terribly unproductive. We have seen too many manufacturers think that a 12 year old will respond favorably to the very same name or package that a 4 year old loves. Let's remember, please, that 2 year olds will cry if their moms don't hug and kiss them, while 16 year olds will "die" if their moms hug and kiss them, especially in public.

This brings us to the primary reason that my associates, Tim Coffey, Greg Livingston, and I decided to write this book. *All kids are definitely not alike.*

Okay, so on whom do we concentrate? Is there a "heart" of the kids' market? Is there one segment of the youth market that wields more influence and power than the others? We think it is the tween.

The *tween*—too old to be a "kid," too young to be a "teen." Too old to want to be totally dependent on parents; too young to have a work permit. Too old to want to be associated with young kids; too young to be allowed into a PG-13 movie.

Yet, tweens are a consumer segment that can create a $100+ million brand.

This book will take a close, detailed look at the tween market—its makeup and its world. It will look at how this group of highly influential consumers has changed over just the past few years and what businesses are doing to attract this important group.

The book will also explore some of the successful ways in which to market to tweens, from research to product development, packaging, and advertising.

SOME BACKGROUND

I thought it would be wise to provide a little background on how and why I developed my passion for youth marketing and why I would persuade myself and my two best friends, Tim and Greg, to risk our marriages and social lives in order to spend more than six months of evenings, weekends, and early mornings working on this book.

About 20 years ago, I had the good fortune of being called by an executive recruiter looking to fill a senior management position at an advertising agency whose primary client was the Kenner Toy Company—one of the industry's largest advertisers.

The agency was in search of a client-side marketing executive who could help "teach" its toy clients the benefits and disciplines of classic consumer package goods marketing. Considering that I was currently marketing such "fun" products as household cleaning products, toilet bowl cleaners, and bathroom fresheners, I gladly traded in that job for the chance to make ads and play with toys.

Like most classically trained consumer package goods marketers, I started the job with a chip on my shoulder. After all, I knew everything about the right way to market products to the consumer of that era—the

American Housewife. I was ready to start working with Kenner's product managers to show them how to analyze their business, write and develop volume forecasts, determine if marketing opportunities existed, and so forth. I actually did help them see and launch several new product line extensions.

But to my big surprise, the Kenner toy company showed me something that few, if any, classic consumer package goods marketing executives were aware of at that time—the power and influence that children had in the American household!

The time was early in the 1980s, and, with few exceptions, the only companies reaching out to the kid's market segment were toy companies, confectionery companies, and, oh yes, one major breakfast cereal company, General Mills, the parent company of my toy client, Kenner. Kenner and other toy companies knew that they could communicate directly to children and motivate them to influence their parents' purchase decisions. The toy industry probably knew, before any other marketer, the power of licensing, and it was among the first to design packaging, advertising, and promotions with the kid in mind.

Wow, what an opportunity! I would spread the word to all of the classic consumer goods manufacturers unaware of this big, powerful, easy-to-reach consumer. By doing so, I would bring in dozens of new clients for my agency and hundreds of millions of dollars in advertising. I was wrong. It was too early. Marketers did not want to hear of such lunacy. Housewives made the purchases. Housewives, and occasionally their husbands, made the decisions.

TIMES HAVE CHANGED

Not only have kids become even more influential and powerful as a consumer base, but many of today's marketers, retailers, and services are now zeroing in on this segment.

A reporter in *The Wall Street Journal* wrote in October 1998, "The rise in children's disposable income, as well as a corresponding rise in children's decision making power, has prompted a fundamental shift in children's buying patterns over the last several years.

"Ten years ago, the majority of marketers didn't see kids as able to absorb complicated messages. . . . Now kids are looked upon as more mature. That's opening up whole new categories."

Actually, the broader interest in youth marketing probably started in 1987 with the book *Children as Consumers: Insights and Implications,* by Dr.

James U. McNeal. This was the first book ever to look at children as a legitimate market of consumers and used all available published research to do so.

This was followed by the first-ever kids' market conference in 1989. According to its organizer, Candi Schwartz, the conference featured 18 speakers and hosted 75 total attendees. Topics were basic, such as package design, radio as a possible kids' medium, and cause-related kids' marketing.

Then in 1992, McNeal released a follow-up book, *Kids as Customers: A Handbook of Marketing to Children,* and marketer's interest in children really took a huge leap. For the first time ever, marketers became aware that kids represented not just one market, but three. McNeal pointed out that children are

- present-day buyers and consumers;
- future consumers who form important branding opinions at an early age and can dramatically impact a company's future earnings once they have grown up; and
- influencers on purchases for their families as well as for themselves.

Perhaps this notion—that kids do not necessarily buy many products themselves but actually influence so many purchases not only for themselves but for their families as a whole—did the most to excite marketers.

McNeal was the first author to attempt to quantify how much children actually influenced family purchases in almost every product category that involved them, not only toys, confectionery, and cereals, but vacations, restaurants, entertainment, and even cars. What he found was that children influenced as much as $130 billion in overall U.S. purchases, or roughly 20 percent of all consumer purchases.

McNeal also pointed out that kids could be segmented into three distinct age groups: preschool, school children, and tweens.

Over the past few years, several more books have addressed this new dynamic market segment. *What Kids Buy and Why,* by Dan Acuff and Robert Reiher, is an excellent book that describes, among other things, how kids' brain development helps to explain why and how they react to certain marketing stimuli. *Creating Evercool,* by Gene Del Vecchio, is a wonderful work on how marketers can keep brands and campaigns fresh, despite the ever-changing world of today's youth. Most recently, McNeal has refreshed his own work with *The Kids Market: Myths and Realities,* which includes comparisons with the Asian market.

Many more well-attended conferences have sprung forth, not only in the United States, but also globally. As a matter of reference, the year 2000 annual global Kid Power Conference attracted more than 50 speakers from such diverse industries as financial, Internet, automotive, and health and beauty aids, among others. More than 300 people attended. Topics included e-commerce, creating brand identity for kids' products, developing kids' products, and more.

Several guidance sources now exist for kid marketing, advertising, and research. Products and services targeted to kids now number in the hundreds, and marketing and advertising spending totals billions of dollars. Throughout this book, we'll explore some of these sources, products, services, and marketing efforts targeted to tweens.

WHO, WHAT, AND WHY OF TWEENS

1

WHO ARE
THESE TWEENS?

In writing this book, we were confronted with the task of challenging our own conventional and intuitive thinking about tweens. First, why should anyone believe that there is such a thing as a tween market anyway? Isn't this just fodder for academics? Okay. So the challenge was not all that difficult. With just a minimum of investigation, you can see that there is definitely something going on with kids in the preadolescent years that makes them different in many ways than younger kids and older teens. In fact, it is a period of phenomenal growth and change and coming of age that is truly miraculous.

Second, why should anyone care? This should be an easy one, too. Today's tween segment is the epicenter of the Baby Boomlet, also known as the Echo Boom, and Generation Y, the last offspring of the large and powerful Baby-Boom generation. Like their parents, today's tweens are an economic force. They are large in number, in charge, and will determine the winners and losers in the marketplace for years to come. In this chapter and throughout this book, we will illustrate how tweens are different from younger and older kids, and we will try to explain why.

WHAT IS A TWEEN?

The first and most elementary question this book has to ask and answer is: Just exactly what is a tween? While at first glance this question seems elementary, the answer is definitely not straightforward. In fact, in our work with many different companies, we have seen marketers use several different definitions. Most market research, including much of the research reported in this book, defines the tween segment as aged 8 to 12. We also encounter marketers who define the segment as aged 7 to 14, aged 8 to 14, aged 9 to 15, and aged 10 to 16. Some even define tweens not as an age group but as a "state of mind."

In a sense, all of these definitions are right if the basis for choosing them is to identify a sizable, definable market that represents an opportunity for the marketer's business. We will, however, explore and define a basis for the tween market that transcends any particular product or category—one based on as much science and fact as possible. The good news is that our studies of the scientific literature, combined with our extensive firsthand observations, reveal a number of markers that clearly and consistently support the existence of a tween market segment that is distinct from kids and teens.

If you were to spend as much time with kids as we do, you would see that there are dramatic differences from age to age and from boy to girl. We often look at the youth market in as little as two-year increments. When talking about market segments, this may seem too refined, and it probably does not meet a marketer's need for critical mass. However, so much change occurs in the development of kids, tweens, and teens, that to do less would be to miss some critical cognitive and behavioral factors that can have huge impact on the results of your marketing efforts.

So let us start by framing the challenge. In this chapter, we will attempt to define the most appropriate age range that defines the tween market segment. While this challenge might seem somewhat academic, we believe it is critical to develop sound parameters as a way of truly understanding tweens, and, thus, effectively marketing to them. By defining the market segment, we will clearly understand how tweens are different from kids on the younger end, and from teenagers on the older end. We will also attempt to describe any subsegments or breaks in the broader tween segment that will further refine our understanding of this group. With this type of definition, we will be better able to explain the practical research and observations that you will find throughout this book.

OUR HYPOTHESIS

You won't have to wait until the end of the chapter, however, for our view of the most practical and substantiated view of the tween segment. That would be at odds with our Procter & Gamble indoctrination to get to the point. Based on our research, as well as our firsthand experience, we believe the tween segment is defined best as children aged 8 to 12. Further, we believe that there is a significant subsegmentation of this group that divides the group into emerging-younger and older-transitioning tweens, with the divide at about age 11.

We have observed this division in magazines, play patterns, attitudes, and other areas. For example, let's take the readership audience of *Disney Adventures* magazine. Eight-year-old kids love this magazine. However, by age 11, kids perceive the magazine as being too young for them. We've also seen several studies, conducted since year 2000, clear evidence that over three-quarters of 8 and 9 year olds feel comfortable talking to their parents about anything, dropping to two-thirds among 10 to 12 year olds, and sadly, continuing to drop into the teen years.

That all tweens are not created equal stands to reason because every single year of a tween's development brings with it sizable changes. An 8 year old is not identical to a 10 year old, and an 8 year old is certainly not like a 12 year old! While only 4 to 5 years separate the upper and lower ages of our tween segment, remember that a 12 year old has experienced 50 percent more in life than an 8 year old. That's like comparing a 60 year old with a 40 year old. It is the abrasion of life's experiences together with some physical development that drives changes in the cognitive development of children.

Remember that a 12 year old has experienced 50 percent more in life than an 8 year old. That's like comparing a 60 year old with a 40 year old.

A caution: Because our "years 8 to 12" tween age definition is an average representation, it is possible that the endpoints are transitions. We believe this transition is most apparent at the younger end of the range, with some 7 year olds showing clear tween characteristics. A number of factors suggest that the break at the top of the age range is clearer and more precise. In the balance of this chapter, we will provide the basis for this thinking.

DEFINING THE WORD *TWEEN*

We see the defining characteristic of tweens as their "split personality" that toggles between kid behaviors and attitudes and those of a teenager.

The first clue to the definition of the tween market segment is the word *tween*. We have not been able to determine who first coined the term or when it was used first. Commonly, however, it is used simply to describe those kids who are "in between" being little kids and being teenagers. This term could not be more appropriate. Repeatedly, we see the defining characteristic of tweens as their "split personality" that toggles between kid behaviors and attitudes and those of a teenager. So, as a descriptor of this segment, the word really works. But what does it tell us about the definition of the segment? If you stick with the language and what it implies about the age range, you can make the case that the upper end of the segment is 12 years old. Age 13, linguistically, is the beginning of the teenage years. This is simple enough. Unfortunately, linguistics fail us at the lower end of the segment. Can we simply assume that 12 years is the most appropriate upper end of the segment just because our language makes a differentiation? It is just not going to be that easy.

What we need is a definition that will reveal to us substantive, predictable, and stable differences between kids on the younger end and teenagers on the older end. If we can not define these kinds of markers, then we have to admit that there is not really a market segment at all. Of course, this is greatly at odds with our real-world, everyday experience, where we see firsthand a unique and interesting group of young people whom many of our clients hold in the highest regard. So, there must be some substance we can identify in order to guide marketers.

PIAGET'S THEORY OF COGNITIVE DEVELOPMENT

Perhaps the most compelling basis for the tween market segment comes from developmental psychologist Jean Piaget (1896–1980). Piaget's work and research, first published in 1924, are a primary foundation of child developmental and educational psychology. Through his research, Piaget developed a comprehensive view of how intelligence develops from infancy through adolescence. He recognized the following four broad stages of cognitive development:

1. The Period of Sensori-Motor Intelligence (0 to 2 years)
2. The Period of Preoperational Thought (2 to 7 years)
3. The Period of Concrete Operations (7 to 11 years)
4. The Period of Formal Operations (11 to 15 years)

In defining these stages of development, Piaget recognized significant differences in the cognitive abilities of children from one age group to the next, although the age ranges given are normative. He posited that the development of intelligence was sequential and driven by a child's experience with the environment. Given this, it is possible that one child could move from one stage to the next at a different rate than another. Also, it suggests the possibility that progression from one stage to the next can be different for individual cultures, and it can change over time if the experiences of children also change. What is fixed is that children must progress from one stage to the next, building on the cognitive abilities gained in earlier stages.

As marketers, it makes sense to use a model of cognitive development to understand the presence of a genuine market segment, as nearly everything we do is concerned with information processing. So, having a better understanding of how children process information about the world around them is at the center of understanding the effectiveness of marketing activities, such as new product development, research, advertising, and promotion.

For our purposes, we will look further at Piaget's Period of Concrete Operations for clues about what differentiates tweens from infants, younger children, and young adolescents. Let us briefly review the defining characteristics of each stage of development.

The Period of Sensori-Motor Intelligence (0 to 2 years)

Piaget describes six stages of the Sensori-Motor child. A newborn child begins life with only simple reflexes: sucking, grasping, crying, and movement of arms, trunk, and head. At this point, the child does not have thoughts or symbolic representations of objects in mind. Intelligence develops as the child interacts with the environment and begins to experience reactions and sensations from reflexive actions. As any parent will attest, infants quickly learn that crying prompts actions on the part of the parent—feeding, changing diapers, entertainment, cuddling, and so forth. Any mother will tell you that infants soon employ different cries for different needs, manifesting early signs of intentionality, and, perhaps, the earliest signs of the "Four-Eyed, Four-Legged consumer," that is, the give-and-take communication and decision-making process that takes place between mother and child that makes them function as one unit.

Through experience and experimentation, the child eventually begins to develop the early signs of thought. By the time children are 2 years old, they are aware of objects separate from themselves, and they can even form an image in their minds of the object in its absence. Further, 2 year olds, unlike a newborn, have the ability to solve problems through a primitive type of creativity. So in a sense, the Sensori-Motor child transforms from a virtual blank slate to a thinking person in the short span of two years.

Our tween Concrete Operational child and the next-phase Preoperational child are vastly different from the Sensori-Motor child in that they will develop primarily based on their ability to think and less so from direct motor or sensory experience.

The Period of Preoperational Thought (3 to 7 years)

In the Preoperational period, the child shifts from interacting with his or her environment through senses and movement to functioning in a conceptual-symbolic mode. The most significant and apparent sign of this new level of cognitive development is the child's use of language, whereby words are used as symbols in place of objects. The first use of language occurs around age 2, and the virtual mastery of the language is complete by age 4. Even though by age 4 a child has the ability to communicate with others, some characteristics of the Preoperational child clearly differentiate him or her from the older Concrete Operational child.

The Preoperational child lacks the cognitive ability to think logically and is still bound by his or her immediate perceptions of reality. Anyone who has dealt directly with children in this age group will tell you they are extremely literal, in the sense that they can only react to what they see. This literalness shows itself clearly when trying to communicate, research, or develop new product concepts for this group. Any kind of sophisticated or complex thinking that adults take for granted can go right over the head of the Preoperational child. Unless you understand and really scrutinize your efforts from a Preoperational child's perspective, you may not know why things aren't working. The main characteristics that hinder the Preoperational child from logical thought are egocentrism and being bound by perception.

For the Preoperational child, *egocentrism* is the inability to take on another's point of view. She is not this way out of rudeness or bad behavior; it is simply the state of the child's cognitive development. She does not conceive that anyone thinks differently from herself. The Preoperational child knows she is always correct, because she does not yet have the ability to reflect on her own thoughts. Next time you encounter an adult with the same characteristics, you might suggest to them that they are very Preoperational today. They won't get it, but you will.

Eventually, at age 6 or 7, or earlier if the child is constantly exposed to other children, egocentrism will be eroded by the conflict of social pressure. Significantly, it is only then that the child begins increasingly to validate his own thoughts against those of his peers. Prior to this, a Preoperational child's play with others is mostly in parallel. Games that have rules are not yet comprehensible to the child at age 4 or 5. Communication is not person to person, but it consists of the child's monologue.

Perhaps the most interesting characteristic of Preoperational children is that they are bound by perceptions. That is, they believe what they see in a rigid and unsuspecting way. Piaget referred to this as the inability to observe or comprehend that an object stays the same even when its outside appearance changes. This cognitive deficiency is in an overall sense the inability to think multidimensionally.

Piaget described several aspects of being bound by perceptions. The first is centration. Said simply, *centration* is the child's tendency to focus on one dimension or feature of an object to the exclusion of others. We have seen this characteristic at work many times when advertising toys to this age range. These younger children will tend to focus on one feature (the flashiest or largest) to the exclusion of all others, much to the chagrin of the toy manufacturer who has worked so hard to load the toy with multiple features. The lesson here for marketers is that you had better identify the most appealing feature or the thrill of the product and focus on that in your advertising and merchandising.

These younger children will tend to focus on one feature (the flashiest or largest) to the exclusion of all others.

The next aspect is that a Preoperational child will focus on states versus transformations. The best way to explain this is to describe the task that Piaget gave to children to demonstrate this characteristic. Piaget held a bar in a straight-up vertical position, and let it fall to horizontal. He then asked the children to choose from a selection of pictures that illustrated the movement of the bar. Despite being shown pictures that illustrated the process of falling with a series of drawings of the bar on the way down, most children chose pictures that showed only the beginning and the end. A commercial that shows a lot of quick-cut action, but has no beginning and ending statement will go over the head of the Preoperational child.

The lack of reversible thinking also demonstrates the Preoperational child's confinement to immediate and literal perceptions, and his or her inability to think or solve problems using logic. *Reversible thinking* is the ability to mentally trace a series of events or line of reasoning from the endpoint back to the beginning. Said another way, children in the Preoperational stage do not easily understand cause and effect relationships. They see the effect and cannot see beyond that immediate perception to remember or comprehend the cause. This is further evidence of the Preoperational child's relatively simplistic information processing abilities.

Through experience and maturation, children will eventually enter a more sophisticated and adult-like state of cognitive development by the time they are age 6 or 7. They will leave behind the egocentrism of the Preoperational Period to enter the Period of Concrete Operations.

The Period of Concrete Operations (7 to 11 years)

The stage that Piaget might have considered the tween segment is the Period of Concrete Operations. It is in this stage that the child first has the cognitive ability to apply logic to concrete problems. The Concrete Operational child has the newfound cognitive power to use both thought and perception to solve problems. No longer bound by perceptions, children in this stage can overcome all of the obstacles to logical thought processes that held them back during the Preoperational Period. In addition, and perhaps most telling about tweens, is that they become nonegocentric in their thinking and communication. This is the beginning of the social being, and, in many ways, this is the child's introduction to the real world.

Much of the cognitive development of the Concrete Operations period has implications for the increasing importance of peers. As egocentric thinking dissolves, children are forced to confront the understanding that others may have ideas and points of view different from their own. Consequently, they now begin to pay attention to the points of view of others as a way to verify their own. Also, other cognitive characteristics emerge that have social implications: seriation and classification.

Seriation is the ability to mentally order elements based on size. Children at this stage have a broader view and capacity to understand who is taller, shorter, thinner, fatter, faster, slower, and so forth. *Classification* is the ability to ascribe values to classes of people, events, and objects. From this ability, it is clear to see how children begin to make judgments about peer groups, products, and experiences. This cognitive capacity, in our estimation, is the foundation of brand understanding beyond mere product features.

Concrete Operational children appreciate and, even prefer, humor with a double-meaning.

The new logical abilities of Concrete Operational children give them a more sophisticated appreciation of humor. They now appreciate and even prefer humor with a double-meaning. The humor, however, should still be obvious and not too subtle. It's the kind of humor that might end with "get it?" We saw this firsthand with our work on Trolli Sour Brite Crawlers gummi worms. This age group loved the idea that "you think I'm actually eating a real worm, but I know I'm not." It's not until the age of 10 or 11 that children can understand and appreciate sarcasm or satire.

The Concrete Operational child also has the ability to follow and master more complex storylines. Some perfect examples are Pokémon cards and the Harry Potter books. Both of these present a wealth of classification challenges that the Concrete Operational child relishes. Preoperational children are left in the dust when it comes to complex storylines. More than a few younger children have been bamboozled out of prized Pokémon cards by older siblings because they did not completely understand the game.

There are limitations, however, to the Concrete Operational child's cognitive abilities that differentiate him or her from the adolescent Formal Operations stage. These limitations are primarily the inability of the Concrete Operational child to deal with abstraction. Children at this age are logical insofar as the subject is based in reality or concreteness. In this sense, they are still somewhat perception bound. We see this characteristic frequently when developing new product concepts. If an idea is totally unique, without some logical reason for being, the Concrete Operational child will reject it. Of course, a kid's logic does not necessarily match an adult's. They will accept created logic, as long as it is not too much at odds with something they already know.

A simple, yet profound way to really understand the difference between concrete and abstract thinking was described to us by Dr. Langbourne Rust, EdD, using the following exercise: Close your eyes and try to visualize something in your mind, say a dog, or flower, or tree. Most of us can see these images in our mind. That is concrete thinking. Now try to visualize something such as . . . truth. The mind goes blank. This is abstract thinking. We have found this distinction to be a useful tool when evaluating advertising for kids. The more concrete, the better when it comes to kids and tweens.

The Concrete Operational child, Piaget's tween, has entered an age of near-adult cognitive abilities. The power of logic and comprehension of new details about their environment jumpstart their curiosity and sense of command of the world around them. Concrete Operational children are generally very positive and energized, as they have not yet experienced the governing sense of self-consciousness that will plague the older teen. But they are acutely interested in ranking, classifying, and being in conformance with their peers.

Concrete Operational children have not yet experienced the governing sense of self-consciousness that will plague the older teen.

The Period of Formal Operations (11 to 15 years)

The Period of Formal Operations is the final stage in Piaget's progression of cognitive development, with the complete logical capabilities of an adult coming to fruition. Unlike the Concrete Operational stage, where children are restricted to dealing with rational and logical manipulation of concrete or reality based concepts, the Formal Operations stage can deal with possibilities, hypotheses, and abstractions. Of course, like all of Piaget's stages, the development of new cognitive abilities happens in phases. So, there is a progression from age 11 to age 15, with complete conceptual and abstract thinking ability available towards the end of the period.

Curiously, Piaget and others identified a new type of egocentrism that emerges in Formal Operational children, and it explains a lot about the kind of behaviors and attitudes commonly associated with young teens. That is, young teens, because of their increased cognitive powers, have the ability to imagine what others may be thinking. Not surprisingly, teens tend to believe that others are thinking about them, and that others are as critical in their thinking as the teens are of themselves.

This new egocentrism is the root of extreme self-consciousness that is typical of teens, and it is a characteristic that differentiates them from tweens. Tweens look for validation of their ideas, beliefs, and choices from others, but they are not yet at the paranoid level that teens are. The tween says, "I am right, but what do you think?" The teen says, "I know you think I'm wrong, so I probably am."

Refocusing on the tweens, their lower level of self-consciousness explains why they are more comfortable toggling between kid-like play behaviors and more teen-like sophistication. When we work with tweens, we see kids who are comfortable with themselves. While tween girls or boys might not bring their Barbies or GI Joes to school because they will get concrete and direct teasing, they still like to play with them at home every once in a while. Teens, on the other hand, reject in their minds and on the behalf of others the notion of anything childish.

Also related to teens' more developed thinking ability is their questioning of adult authority and the end of seeing their parents as the source of absolute truth. Partly because of their cognitive prowess and partly because of their increasing awareness of the fact that they will have to take care of themselves someday soon, teens question everything their parents stand for. The early teen years are marked by the withdrawal from family, as a step towards

The early teen years are marked by the withdrawal from family, as a step towards independence.

independence. On the other hand, tweens do not yet have such developed intellectual powers nor, yet, a view towards their independence from their parents. As a result, family is still important to them.

DOES PIAGET TELL US EVERYTHING WE NEED TO KNOW?

When it comes to identifying the older and younger ends of the tween segment, Piaget's classifications are extremely helpful, but do they represent the best break points for the practical world of marketing? We believe the answer is no. From the real-world perspective, we think that it makes the most sense to lag Piaget's break points by one year to ensure that the dominant characteristics of the tween group are more fully formed. So, instead of simply classifying the tween segment as beginning at 7 and ending at 11, we prefer using 8 to 12.

Having put our stake in the ground, we must state the inevitable, but important, caveat. That is, cognitive development progresses from immature to mature in terms of capabilities and characteristics common to a given stage. Think of this as if a child is climbing up one side of the cognitive mountain towards the peak of developmental maturity in a particular stage. Then he or she goes down the other side as the characteristics of the next stage begin to emerge. This way of thinking is the basis for our model of the tween market as two subsegments—the emerging tween and the transitioning tween. We put the peak—or dividing line—of the tween segment beginning at age 11.

Our experience in marketing to tweens first suggested to us that something significant happens around age 11 that alters the preferences and perceptions of tweens. Many products aimed at tweens seemed to lose favor after the age of 10. Some examples are fruit snacks, juice drinks, and many toys. These categories seem to fall off the cliff with older tweens. This same break also occurs in television programming, with younger tweens preferring *Rugrats*, while older tweens prefer *Friends*.

Many products aimed at tweens seemed to lose favor after the age of 10.

Researchers have also documented changes that occur at this age that relate to increasing maturity of social skills and understanding. The most interesting is research on the Stages of Friendship. This research shows that children's ideas about friendship change from the early elementary school through middle school years. The stages of friendship are as follows:

- *Level 1.* Friendship as a handy playmate (about age 5 to 7 years). Friends are simply those with whom one frequently plays. There is no sense of liking or disliking another person based on personality traits.
- *Level 2.* Friendship as mutual trust and assistance (about 8 to 10 years). Mutual trust is the defining element of friendship at this stage. Not only do we do things together, but we can also count on each other for support.
- *Level 3.* Friendship as intimacy and mutual understanding (age 11 to 15 and older). Friends understand and accept one another and share innermost thoughts and feelings. The depth of the relationship supports loyalty and stability.

There are also physical characteristics of 8 to 12 year olds that differentiate them from younger kids and teenagers, and help explain the subsegmentation that occurs at age 11. This may seem like obvious stuff, but the physical characteristics of tweens have a huge impact on how they relate to the world. Do you know how tall the average tween boys or girls are? How much they weigh? What other physical characteristics might have an effect on how they perceive the world?

The charts in Figure 1.1 and Figure 1.2 illustrate the average heights and weights of boys and girls aged 0 to 20 years. Some key points are that tween boys and girls are pretty close together in both height and weight, with the exception of age 12, when girls are somewhat bigger than boys are. It is not until after age 12 that boys' size permanently outpaces girls'. On average, tweens grow from about 50 inches (4 ft. 2 in.) to 60 inches (5 ft.) in height and from 55 pounds to 88 pounds from ages 8 to 12.

Anyone who designs retail space where tween products will be sold needs to take these numbers into consideration. We've seen some savvy marketers who size their stores to make tweens feel like they are most important. Check out a Limited Too store, and you'll find they have designed every detail to make the tween girl feel special. Then compare it with Gap Kids, which is more mom-centric. Where would you rather shop if you were 4 feet tall?

Perhaps the most important physical event in the life of a tween is the initial onset of puberty. On average, both boys and girls show early signs of puberty at about age 11. For girls, this includes the budding of the breasts. For boys, it is the enlargement of the testes. Both boys and girls show an increase in the velocity of height and weight gain at around age 11.

FIGURE 1.1

Stature-for-Age and Weight-for-Age Percentiles, Girls 2 to 20 years

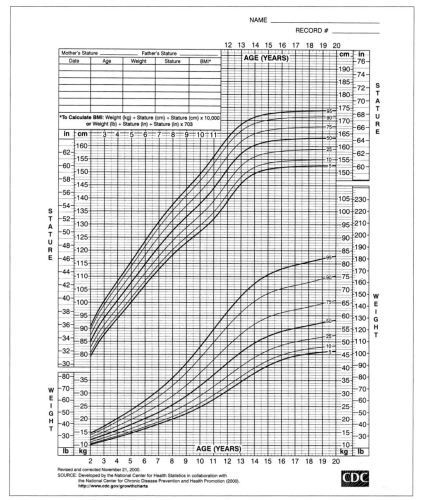

Source: CDC Growth Charts: United States, Centers for Disease Control & Prevention, National Center for Health Statistics, May 30, 2000

The beginning of puberty, even in its early stages, sets off an increase in sexual identities. Boys want to become more masculine and girls want to become more feminine. With the physical changes of puberty, it is possible that there are changes in other senses. Do their taste buds change? How about their sense of smell? We don't know for sure, but we have seen some evidence to suggest these changes may occur.

FIGURE 1.2

Stature-for-Age and Weight-for-Age Percentiles, Boys 2 to 20 years

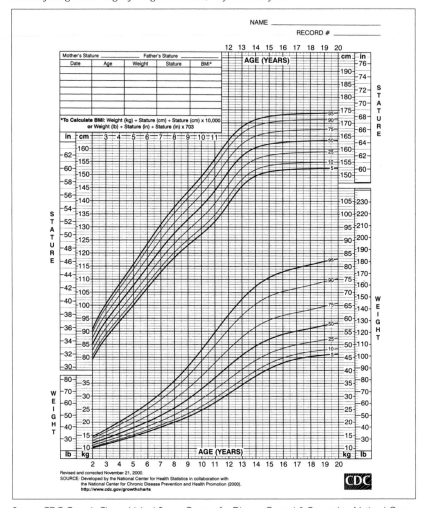

Source: CDC Growth Charts: United States, Centers for Disease Control & Prevention, National Center for Health Statistics, May 30, 2000

TWEENS TODAY VERSUS TWEENS YESTERDAY

"Tweens today are different." "No, they are the same as they've been for generations." We hear this argument often. In fact, both tween generations are the same in many ways—physiologically and psychologically. Certainly, Piaget teaches us that the stages of cognitive development

FIGURE 1.3

Growth Curves of Different Organ Systems of the Body

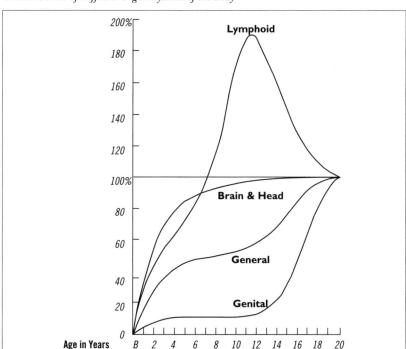

Source: from J. M. Tanner, *Growth in Adolescence*, 2nd edition, Blackwell, Oxford 1962

have been recognized for at least 75 years! However, in many ways tweens are different today.

What makes today's tweens different from tweens of the past is their experiences. Experiences teach. Moreover, from these learnings, we change the way we interpret the world and the way we act. It has been said that "experience is the best teacher. First you get the test, then you get the lesson."

What are some of the things that are different today? Families are more fluid and fractured. Schools teach more than just the 4 Rs. Technology is a way of life. New economic realities exist. Logos are on everything. Heroes are fragile. Schools can be dangerous, and cultural diversity is good. As we'll see later in the chapter, today's tweens have been subjected to the defining events and circumstances that differ significantly from the experiences of prior generations.

Until the mid-1990s, most modern tweens had Baby Boomer parents. But that is changing too. Most tweens today and virtually all tweens in a few years will have Gen-X parents. Gen Xers, the generation after the

Baby Boom, were born between 1965 and 1976. They began having babies at the median age of about 24 and are now just starting to become the parents of tweens.

Are Gen Xers going to be different parents than those of the past? Will they teach their tweens different values? While no one can be certain, there are many indications that Gen Xers are and will continue to raise their children differently than their Boomer predecessors. Unlike Boomer parents, Gen Xers themselves were raised in a much more risk-saturated, unstable world. Virtually everything had consequences: sex could mean AIDS; drugs could mean addiction. They lived in two households, Mom's and Dad's.

Some Gen Xers who are now parents were raised by Baby Boomers. Gen Xers were children during times marked by high divorce rates, latch-key kids, homelessness, national debt, ozone deterioration, downsizing, and layoffs. Even when they came from very stable homes, they were surrounded by examples of what not to do as parents. Gen Xers will be parents who have learned that they can take nothing for granted. Unlike Boomers, who felt that their job was their life, Gen Xers want a good job and a good life, with the following significant consequences:

- *Today's and tomorrow's tweens are more likely to have stay-at-home moms or other relatives to care for them and mold them.* We have already begun to see this in the workforce. A surprising number of our young moms on staff want to switch to part-time positions so they can be home with their children, and we know of at least some stay-at-home dads as well.

  One of our daughters, a trailing Gen Xer, told us that many of her girlfriends say there is "no way" that they will not stay home for at least the first several years of their children growing up. She said that even her boyfriends have said that either their wives or they themselves will stay home with their children during the first several years.

- *Tweens will probably be savvier consumers at an even younger age.* Gen Xers have grown up to be much savvier consumers than their Boomer predecessors and will probably make sure that their children are as well. In many of today's focus groups we hear young moms express that they are trying to encourage and teach their children to make educated product choices at very young ages. They even ask their children's opinions!

- *They will have a greater knowledge of the importance of ecology.* Gen Xers have seen the results of the poor ecological planning among their predecessors and will teach, through example, that recycling and other environmental steps are good.

To find out more about how today's tweens are different than those of even the most recent past, we talked to some of today's tweens and teens ("yesterday's" tweens). These tweens and teens saw lots of differences. Here's just a sample of what we heard.

One of the biggest changes between today's tweens and those of just a few years ago involves their day-to-day experiences with computer technology. What's interesting is that even though most of today's teens accept computer technology as a fact of life, they envy their younger cohort's superiority in this area.

> *Computers are evil, I hate them! It's not fair. How come she (younger sister) knows so much more about the computer?*
>
> **—14-year-old girl**

What a difference only two years can make!

Today's tweens not only have access to home PCs, but they have access to the best PCs in their house.

> *We used to have one computer, but then we got a second one. I only use the new one because it's so much faster. Our old computer was slow to get on the Internet, too. Now we have Zoomtown [high-speed Internet access]. It's great because I can use the phone and be on the Internet at the same time!*
>
> **—13-year-old boy**

Another very important difference between today's tween and yesterday's tween is their experiences with advanced telephone technology and communication. Now, everyone wants or has a cell phone. It is the ultimate accessory.

> *When I was 12, I really, really wanted a pager. I looked at a lot and finally got the one I liked. Now today's kids want a cell phone!*
>
> **—15-year-old girl**

> *We have two cell phones in my family. My dad uses his mostly for work, and my mom gives me hers when I go out. I'm supposed to call her and let her know where I am.*
>
> **—12-year-old girl**

Another area of tween communication that has grown astronomically over the last year or two is instant messaging—or IMing. Although older tweens have adopted this form of communicating with each other, tweens are absolutely addicted. It is not unheard of for tweens to have 50 or 60 buddies in their list, some of whom they may not even know.

> *I have so many buddies on my list I have to use several screen names to fit them all in. Some of the people are friends of my friends so it's a good way to meet new people. I love IMing. It's so cool.*
>
> **—12-year-old girl**

E-mailing is huge for tweens. Often the very first thing kids do when they get home from school is to check their e-mail. What a disappointment it is when there is no "You've got mail" waiting for you. It's a sign of how popular you are to get lots of messages.

> *I check my e-mail at least once every day—sometimes more.*
>
> **—13-year-old boy**

> *I can't wait to see how many messages are waiting for me.*
>
> **—11-year-old girl**

Older teens tell us that they see a lot more emphasis put on designer clothing today. It doesn't seem to matter if the designer is super expensive either; tweens still want it.

> *The coat I want is from North Face. It costs $479. It's the only coat I want.*
>
> **—14-year-old girl**

> *I think younger kids are more into the designer label—I know what I like, and it doesn't HAVE to be from Abercrombie. I mean, who wants to look like everyone else?*
>
> **—16-year-old girl**

> *My younger sister (12) seems to be much more concerned with trendy brands. It's like there is this pressure to fit in, much more than when I was her age.*
>
> **—18-year-old girl**

It's only been within the last few years that stores or even departments within stores have begun to truly cater to the tween-age group.

Tween girls want to discover their own look—somewhere between dress-up glam and everyday fun fashion.

> *I first discovered I liked shopping when I actually found a store I liked and clothes that fit and that I liked.*
>
> **—11-year-old girl**

> *I like to go shopping for ME.*
>
> **—8-year-old girl**

The social pressures of "going-out" seem to have accelerated as well. Older teens tell us that their younger siblings seem to be much more caught up with having boyfriends or girlfriends.

> *Sixth graders [about 11 years old] are pairing up and "going out" and girls are trying to take away their best friends' boyfriends. I hear them talking about how to make that first kiss be so right!*
>
> **—19-year-old girl**

One point that becomes crystal clear is that technology is advancing so quickly that even tweens start to feel a bit outdated by the time they are teens.

WHAT WILL THEY BE WHEN THEY GROW UP?

All marketers should be asking themselves this question: "What will tweens be when they grow up?" After all, today's tweens will be tomorrow's prime consumers of everything under the sun. For the past 40 years, Baby Boomers have defined the fortunes and failings of many brands and companies. That's because Boomers were a population force of a size never seen before. Now, it is the turn of their children and grandchildren.

Baby Boomers, at a later age than generations before them, have spawned a large and powerful group of children, sometimes referred to the Echo Boomers or Generation Y. Also called Millennials, they are already the drivers of the new economy. Today's tweens are part of this group. Marketers who understand them now and keep up with where they are going will have a competitive advantage. Those who don't may become their father's Oldsmobile—out of sync and out of business.

So, to help you avoid that shameful and career-limiting demise, we will attempt to forecast the future consumer behaviors of today's tweens. To do this, we will look at some significant events in the lives of today's tweens that may shape their values, attitudes, and behaviors in the years to come. Indeed, every generation seems to have some defining events and circumstances from their formative years that have a profound influence on them as adults.

INFLUENCES ON GENERATION Y

In their book *Rocking the Ages*, Smith and Clurman describe a model of how life stage, current conditions, and formative cohort experiences influence the development of values, preferences, and marketplace behaviors. They also claim that the formative cohort experiences were the most influential factor in defining the unique characteristics of each successive generation. (See Figure 1.5.)

FIGURE 1.5
Generational Influences

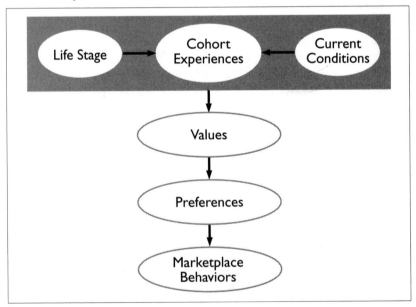

Generational Influence Model

Smith and Clurman analyzed the current adult generations—Matures, aged 65+; Boomers, now aged 37 to 55; and Gen Xers, now aged 25 to 36. By looking retrospectively at the defining events that occurred in the formative years of these generations, they felt that one could better understand each group's current characteristics.

Now, we will do something much more difficult. That is, we will look at some of the defining experiences of the last several years, as a way of predicting the adult characteristics of today's tweens. Inarguably, tweens are right now experiencing their formative years. As a result, today's current events are those that will likely shape their values, preferences, and marketplace behaviors as adults.

Let's briefly look at how some of the key events in the lives of previous generations relate to their current characteristics as adults. (See Figure 1.6.)

Given that significant events have an influence on the future characteristics of generations, what events will influence the future behavior of today's tweens? Knowing the key events that have influenced previous generations, when we look at the events of the last several years, we see some striking occurrences that will undoubtedly affect today's tweens for many years to come. (See Figure 1.7.)

As you can see, the events of the last several years have been quite a bit different than those of previous generations. Of course, the terrorist attacks of September 11 were, for all of us, horrific and will surely mark time. Sadly, when viewed in the continuum of events since the mid-90s,

FIGURE 1.6

Key Events Affecting Previous Generations

AGE	COHORT	KEY EVENTS	INFLUENCES
65+	Matures	Depression World War II	Duty Team player
37 to 55	Boomers	Vietnam The 1960s Strong economy	Individuality Entitlement
25 to 36	Gen Xers	Recession Rightsizing Terrorism AIDS	Diversity Savvy Entrepreneur

FIGURE 1.7
Key Events Affecting Today's Tweens

1996	Clinton re-elected president by a landslide
	The bombing of the Atlanta Summer Olympics
	TWA Flight 800 explodes in the air
	Beanie Babies
1997	Princess Diana killed in a car crash while being chased by photographers
	Cloning of sheep
	Timothy McVeigh convicted as Oklahoma City bomber
	Giga Pets
1998	Clinton/Monica Lewinsky scandal
	Viagra for impotence advertised on TV
	Mark McGuire hits 70 home runs
	John Glenn goes to space again at age 70
	Furby is the hot toy
1999	Millennium bug
	Millennium doomsayers
	Clinton impeached with record high job approval ratings
	Columbine school shootings
	JFK Jr. dies in plane crash
	Economy on fire/Internet stocks
	Pokémon craze
2000	Year 2000 happens with no problems
	Government sends Elian Gonzales back to Cuba
	U.S. presidential election indecision
	Harry Potter books rule
	Razor Scooters the new craze
2001	September 11 WTC and Pentagon attacks
	War in Afghanistan
	Anthrax scares
	Harry Potter movie opens
	Reality shows and game shows are staples on TV
	File swapping at the center of legal battles
2002	Washington D.C. sniper attacks
	War in Afghanistan
	Catholic Church sex scandal
	Corporate scandal at Enron, Arthur Andersen, Merrill Lynch, WorldCom, Global Crossing, Citigroup, and Kmart
	Spider-Man a big hit at the box office

September 11 could be viewed as an acceleration of an already well-established trend of local threat and violence.

The $64,000 question, or should we say the million-dollar challenge, is what impact will these events have on today's tweens as they reach adulthood. First, we will try to synthesize the nature and character of the events as a way of focusing on the major themes. As we see it, there are several trends worth noting.

- *Global peace/local violence.* Today's tweens have lived in a world that is not experiencing broad-based war or divisions. Communism is gone. Russia is our friend. The only issue is whether the Russians can get their economy together. The threat now is from within our own country or our own school. Clearly, the wars in Afghanistan and Iraq have been intensely covered in the media, but, still, the global situation is relatively static when compared with previous generations who lived under the constancy of the Cold War or true world wars. The threat of local violence is changing the way our children play and their general feeling of security.

- *Fallen and infallible heroes.* Nobody is perfect anymore. Our political leaders have morality issues. Sports and entertainment figures are regularly indicted for violence and drug abuse. Recently, corporate leaders have also fallen from grace. All of this moral turpitude has created an emotional void that must be filled. Currently, that void is driving the popularity of such fantasy heroes as Spider-Man, with more coming soon. Fortunately, these tweens have also seen real heroes in action in the event and aftermath of September 11.

- *The complex family.* No generation ever before has grown up with such high levels of divorce, single-parent households, culturally blended families, and alternative families. It is clear from many studies that children who grow up in a nontraditional family, at the least, face some difficult challenges that will shape their attitudes and values now and in the future.

- *Everybody wants to be a millionaire.* The unprecedented wealth created by the new economy has resulted in tremendous affluence among tweens in the United States. Having lots and lots of money is becoming an expectation. While this trend is still present, both the faltering economy and the influence of Generation-X parents, who are less obsessed with rising above the previous generation, may ultimately lead to a different trend of "greater value on quality of life."

- *The world is at my fingertips.* Today's tweens are right at the epicenter of the Internet and its applications in the home and at school. The Internet has changed the way they communicate with each other. It has changed the way they do schoolwork. It has changed the way they shop. It has changed the way they listen to music.

They have much more power over their immediate world than any previous generation had.

So, what will these realities mean to tweens as they grow up? How might they affect their values and behaviors as consumers, parents, and voters? Following are several key values that we predict will be the natural consequence of the world in which these tweens have grown up.

Control Freaks

We believe that all of the above-mentioned trends will lead to an adult consumer who wants *control*. They have grown up in a world that is both out of control (social) and strikingly in control (personal). It seems likely that they will want to extend the control they have had over their personal environment to as much as is possible to deal with what will likely be a perpetually tumultuous world at large. Mass customization and microtargeted products and services will be the expectation. The opportunity to personalize will be strongly preferred. From a political point-of-view, this generation will seek more voice in their government, not unlike the voice they have over Nickelodeon's Kids Choice Awards or the next new color of M&Ms. Will this result in representatives tapping into the direct and immediate opinions of their constituents' via the Internet on the floor of the House of Representatives? This would not be too far-fetched given the world these kids have experienced and the technology that is already in place.

Good Citizens of the World

In the aftermath of September 11, today's tweens witnessed and felt a deep sense of patriotism and national empathy for those who suffered. This is the kind of experience that etches values into the psyche and that will serve as guidance all their lives. In schools, it is not uncommon for kids to be required to perform community service projects. Add to this today's tweens stronger exposure and opportunity to relate to peers from around the globe, and the result is a strong sense of world citizenship. The effects of this could be far-reaching. We believe this will lead these tweens to become more spiritually connected to their world. This may result in both some obvious things, such as religious affiliation, and some not so obvious things, such as increased environmentalism. It may also fuel a continuance of more traditional family values practiced by their Gen-X parents.

Savvy Consumers

While Gen Xers have been characterized as cynical consumers, today's tweens will transform cynicism into savvy. They will possess a virtual hardwired predisposition of mistrust of any and all products, services, people, and politicians. They have been taught since elementary school to question sources and to evaluate claims. The Internet allows for testimonials of real people, but even these will come under scrutiny if they are exposed as being manipulated by corporations. Brands whose essence is based on trustworthiness will excel. Marketing to these consumers will require approaches that allow for comparison and trial, and alignment with personal values and emotions beyond the product-consumer transaction.

Certainly, any of the above conclusions could turn out to be prophetic or pathetic, depending on how today's tweens internalize the events of the day, and whether there are new, more significant events that happen during the next several years. Just after the publishing of the first edition of this book, we suffered the tragedy of September 11. So, the possibility that significant, life-changing events could still unfold is virtually a given. We can only say that in watching and studying today's tweens, they are optimistic and well-prepared for what lays ahead.

SUMMARY

We have defined the tween age group, for marketing purposes, as beginning at age 8 and ending at age 12. This age group is markedly different from younger kids and older teens in their cognitive, social, and physical development. Cognitively, they are emerging logical thinkers. Socially, they compare themselves to others and are motivated to determine what is right, what is wrong, what is in, and what's out. Their friendships begin as mutual support and evolve to greater depth and intimacy. Physically, they grow like weeds—some 10 inches and 30 pounds almost overnight. Puberty begins their transition to becoming teenagers at about age 11, and along with these physical changes, their view of the world changes substantially.

Today's tweens are different from those of the past because of their childhood experiences and the events now having an impact on their lives. They warrant additional attention if we are to understand better how to market to them now and in the future.

2

WHY BOTHER WITH
THE TWEEN MARKET?

Tweens may be interesting, but does that mean they need special attention? Why should marketers and advertisers put down their *Advertising Age, Money Magazine,* or even *TV Guide* to take the time to learn about this group? Here's why.

The tween segment is the heart of the kids market. Its starting age occurs when kids begin social reading in earnest—meaning that they are beginning to tune in to kids magazines. It is about the time in which the left hemisphere of children's brains is rapidly developing—giving them the power of reason and the mental capacity to understand marketing communications. It is the time in which peer pressure becomes a factor in a person's life and when the urge to grow and become independent and become "not a kid" takes hold.

One of the most important reasons for marketers to study and target tweens is that it is at this stage in their lives when branding begins to take effect. Of the 9 to 11 year olds surveyed in the 2003 Yankelovich Youth MONITOR, 71 percent reported that they tend to stick with a product or brand that they like. Tweens have a growing concern to fit in and to be accepted by their peers. Any item that they wear or consume in front of peers becomes a potential risk. Therefore, kids at this age are particularly concerned that they wear and consume the "right" brands in order to gain the acceptance of their peers.

71 percent reported that they tend to stick with a product or brand that they like.

MARKET SEGMENTS	
Hispanics	35.3 million
African Americans	34.7 million
Asians	10.2 million
U.S. Tweens	**20.9 million**

Source: 2000 U.S. Census

Most importantly, it is the time when, because of earning power, mental power, social pressure, perceived needs, and heightened interest in their world, they probably have the most significant influence on household and family purchases. As professor James U. McNeal says, tweens are the "powerhouse of the kids market."

In Basic Marketing 101, we learn that a market segment is worth targeting if it

- is large enough,
- has significant purchasing power,
- has unique needs, and
- is relatively easy to reach.

The size of the U.S. tween market (8 to 12 year olds) is 20.9 million strong—about two-thirds the size of the entire population of Canada (31.3 million). It is also nearly two-thirds the size of the African American or Hispanic market segments in the United States.

TWEEN DEMOGRAPHICS

Tweens today are more culturally diverse than previous generations, and, because of this diversity and changes in education and media, today's tweens are more accepting of cultural diversity than were their older predecessors. While today's tweens are still mostly white, fewer are white than in their parents' generation. Only 69 percent of tweens, compared with 75 percent of the total U.S. population, classify themselves as "white alone." Moreover, in looking at the cultural mix of the future tween generation, one can see this diversity increasing further.

CULTURAL MAKEUP

Percentage of U.S. Tweens Compared to Overall Population

	Tweens	Total Population
White	69%	75%
Hispanic	16	12
African American	15	12
Asian	3	4

Source: 2000 U.S. Census

Spending Power

Because of the significant influence tweens have over total household expenditures, their true spending power is huge. Looking at year 2000 U.S. Census figures, we project there to be about 9 million families with tweens present, and these families spend about $500 billion a year.

Tweens, themselves, account for at least a quarter trillion dollars in estimated spending. Our research finds tweens spend approximately $11 billion annually on their own. Using the USDA report, Expenditures on Children by Families, we find that tween parents spend an additional $176 billion on them. Lastly, if we assume that tweens further influence is a conservative 20 percent of other family purchases such as vacations, automobiles, restaurant visits, parental clothing and accessories, and so forth, approximately $74 billion more can be attributed to tween influence.

Tween Needs Are Truly Special

Tweens need special sizes of many items, such as clothing, food, and packaging, to fit their respective frame-sizes, and they have a special need to have products made "just for them." As you will see throughout this book, tweens do not want to think of themselves as younger children and, therefore, will not want to use the same products they perceive as being made for "babies." However, equally important, they also know that they are not adults, or for that matter, older teens. They want their products to reflect their interests. Tweens are particular about where they shop and which brands they are willing to use and wear in front of their friends.

Tweens do not want to think of themselves as younger children and, therefore, will not want to use the same products they perceive as being made for "babies."

Tweens Can Be Targeted

Many media vehicles allow for the relatively easy and efficient targeting of today's tweens. Kids print such as *Disney Adventures, Sports Illustrated for Kids,* and *Nickelodeon;* kids TV and radio; special kid-targeted Web sites; and special events are all excellent vehicles. In fact, the tween market segment is one of the least expensive consumer segments to target from a cost-per-thousand perspective.

ARE THEY OVER-MARKETED?

Tweens are starting to be noticed in the general media.

They are (Gen Y) the first generation to come along that's big enough to hurt a boomer brand by simply giving it the cold shoulder . . . companies hoping to win their wallets will have to think like they do.

—Business Week (2/15/99)

Most marketers realize that to be successful in reaching any generation, you must try to think the way that they do. What is new, however, is that it is harder to do this when it comes to thinking the way that today's kids are thinking. We, the authors, have been marketing to kids for over 20 years, and we believe it is more important than ever before to be in continual touch with today's kids. Today's tweens are exposed to so much media, so much learning, so much technology, and, most importantly, so much marketing. They learn from every previous buying experience they've had. There is no way for any of us to predict how they will react to the next new product offering or the next ad campaign.

For example, in recent focus groups, tween reaction to a new product concept for a technologically new communication device and Web site was surprisingly underwhelming. Even though the device and the site were new, they weren't new enough. Even six months earlier the products would have been perceived as being unique. But, in today's world, with so many technological products being launched to serve the teen and tween segments, our tween target saw this new concept as ho-hum.

Ad campaigns thought of as highly creative by some agency creative teams are often now being met with glazed-eyes in focus group and one-on-one viewings. Been there. Done that. Seen that. Heard that. Whew! It's getting tough out there. One of our tweens recently admonished us when viewing one of our intended ad campaigns, saying, "Don't you know, you can't have an ad saying [or implying] 'buy me, buy me, buy me.' It has to be cool and fun. If we like your ad, then we'll like your product."

If we like your ad, then we'll like your product.

In several quantitative new product concept tests, we find it easier to attract moms to new kid-product ideas than it is to attract kids. Many times, we find moms think an idea is unique only to find that their kids think of that same idea as old and boring. This is very dangerous because, as we explain later, it is usually the kid who is the ultimate gatekeeper.

What is happening in the marketplace to cause this rapidly changing, almost cynical response on the part of tweens? Tweens are being saturated with new products and new ad campaigns as never before, and, as you will see in Chapter 7, today's schools are doing their part to make sure that tweens learn to be skeptical regarding advertising messages.

Let's see how many brands and products today's kids are exposed to: When it comes to clothing, Gap Kids, Limited Too, Old Navy, Ralph Lauren for Kids, and dELiA*s Catalog quickly come to mind. Just recently, retailers such as Wal-Mart and Target have also started advertising their clothing lines to kids. As for grocery items, a quick look through our local grocery store found the products shown in Figure 2.1.

It is not just the *numbers* of products to which today's kids are exposed but the types of products now being marketed to them as well. For example, today's kids have not only the chance to buy cute, toy animals that walk but also robotic dogs that do everything but pee. They not only have the opportunity to buy video gaming systems but also PlayStation 2 and the Nintendo GameCube—complete systems that interact with the

FIGURE 2.1

Tween-Oriented Items in Local Supermarket

This is a partial list of products we found in our local grocery store that seem to be marketing to kids, either through packaging, promotions, or advertising.

HEALTH AND BEAUTY AIDS

Sunscreens

Coppertone Kids Sport	Coppertone Kids Spectra 3	Banana Boat Kids Spray

Hair Dyes

got2be Temporary Hair Color	Hair FX Hair Mascara

Shampoos

Pert Kids	Suave Kids	L'Oreal Kids
Hair FX	got2be	Johnson & Johnson Kids

Body Soap

L'Oreal Kids	Johnson & Johnson Kids	Scooby Doo
Harry Potter	Funny Colored Foam	

Bubble Bath

Barbie Rapunzel	Disney Princesses	Power Puff Girls
Harry Potter	Mr. Bubble	Scooby Doo

(continued)

FIGURE 2.1
Continued

Hand Soaps
SoftSoap Foam Works   J & J Kids Super Sudser and
                       Foam Blaster

Hair Accessories
Scunci Girl   Seventeen   Victoria
Goody   Scunci Kids   Cosmopolitan
Karina   Goody Girl

Cosmetics
Bonne Bell Lip Smackers   Fan-Tastics   Charming Lip Gloss
Jane   L.A. Girl   Heaven

Lip Balms
Coppertone Little Licks   Coppertone Natural Fruit   ChapStick Flava Craze
Blistex Fruit Smoothies

Toothbrushes
Colgate Barbie, Looney   Crest Spin Brush   Reach Plaque Buster Harry
 Toons, Disney/Pixar   Spiderman, race car, cell   Potter and others
 characters, PowerPuff   phone, and others   Oral-B Kid Brush
 Girls, Pokémon, and Lego

Toothpastes
Colgate 2-in-1 Toothpastes   AquaFresh, Oral-B Buzz   Reach SpongeBob, Scooby
 Looney Toons, Barbie,   Lightyear, and the Disney   Doo, and Rocket Power
 PowerPuff Girls, Disney/   Princesses fruit and
 Pixar Bubble Fruit   bubblegum flavors
Crest Kids Extreme Flavors

Adhesive Bandages
Nexcare Active Brights,   Band-Aid Brand in Harry   Jimmy Neutron, and
 Bug Collection, Pop-Art,   Potter, Scooby Doo,   Rocket Power
 and Tattoo Wild and   Barbie, SpongeBob,
 Cool Collections   Rugrats, Stars and Stripes,

Kids' Medicines and Vitamins
Children's Chloraseptic   Honey Cough   Simply Cough/Stuffy
Children's Advil/Motrin   Children's Tylenol   Triaminic
PediaCare   Children's Benedryl   Dimetapp and Get Better
Children's Sudafed   Claritin Liquid/Reditabs   Bears
Bugs Bunny Vitamins   Flinstone's Vitamins   Centrum Kids
Little Colds   Little Noses   Children's Kaopectate
Children's Mylanta   One-A-Day Kids   Little Tummys
Vitaball   Children's NyQuil   TheraPatch
                                                  Vick's Pediatric

FIGURE 2.1
Continued

FOODS AND BEVERAGES

Apple Sauces and Fruit Cups

Mott's Fruitsations	Del Monte Fruit and Gel	Fruit Blasters Applesauce
Mott's Hawaiian Punch Applesauce	Cups	Dole Fruit Cups

Cookies and Crackers

Munch 'ems	Cheese Nips	Oreo
Nilla Wafers	Goldfish Crackers	Smucker's Smackers
Chips Ahoy	Teddy Grahams	

Macaroni and Cheese

Kraft Easy Mac, Crazy Noodles, Sponge Bob, and Scooby Doo	Stouffer's Macaroni

Meal Bowls

Hormel Kid's Kitchen	Chef Boyardee Bowls

Pasta Products

Ragu Express	Franco American	Chef Boyardee

Condiments

Heinz EZ Squirt Ketchup

Sweetened Cereals

Froot Loops	Cocoa Pebbles	Lucky Charms
Fruity Pebbles	Honeycomb	Cinnamon Toast Crunch
Frosted Cheerios	Cap'n Crunch	Apple Jacks
Frosted Flakes	Trix	S'morz

Cereal Bars

General Mills Milk 'n Cereal Bars	Kellogg's Cereal and Milk Bars	Quaker Oatmeal Breakfast Squares

Breakfast Pastries

Pop Tarts Pastry Swirls, Snak Stix and Yogurt Blasts	Toaster Strudels and Scrambles	Quaker Oatmeal Toastables

Cheese Products

Kraft Singles, String Cheese, Cheese Cubes, and Handi-Snacks	Sargento String Cheese, Cheese Cubes, Cheese Snacks, and Cheese Twirls

Peanut Butter

Skippy EZ Squeeze and Jar Peter Pan	Skippy Squeeze Stix Reese's	Smucker's Goober

(continued)

FIGURE 2.1
Continued

Flavored Instant Drinks

| Kool-Aid | Ovaltine | Nesquick |
| Flavor-Aid | | |

Pudding and Gelatin

| Jell-O Pudding Cups | Kraft Handi-Snacks | Jell-O Cups |
| Hunt's Snack Packs and Squeeze and Go Pudding | | |

Yogurt

| Dannon Sprinkl'ins | Dannon Danimals Super Creamy, Drinkable, and Squeezable | Yoplait Yumsters, Go-gurt, and Trix |

Fruit Snacks

| Brach's Fruit Snacks and Fruit Rippers | General Mills Fruit by the Foot, Fruit Gushers, and Fruit Roll-ups | Del Monte Fruit Snacks Sunkist Fruit Snacks Jell-O Fruit Snacks |

Soups

Campbell's Fun Favorites Mega Noodle, Chicken Goldfish pasta, Fun Shapes Dinosaur, and others

Lunchables

Fun Fuel	Fun Pack	Taco Bell
Mega Pack	Sandwiches	Cracker Stackers
Fun Snacks	Waffles	

Ice Cream and Novelties

| Nestle Crunch Ice Cream Drumsticks Winnie-the-Pooh Frozen Treats | Popsicle Lick-A-Color, Creamsicles, Fudgesicle, Intense Fruit Shots, and others | Philly Swirls Ice Cream Sandwiches |

Chicken Nuggets

| Tyson Chicken Nuggets | Maple Leaf Farms Chicken Nuggets | Swanson Chicken Nuggets |

Waffles and Pancakes

| Pillsbury Mini-Pancakes, Waffles, and Waffle Sticks | Eggo Waffles and Pancakes | |

Kids TV Dinners

| Swanson Kids Meals | Kid Cuisine Meals | Stouffer's Maxaroni |

Drinks in Portable Containers

Tang	Kool-Aid Kool Bursts, Jammers, and Coolers	Minute Maid Juice Drinks
Hi-C	Sunny Delight	Welch's Juice
Hershey's Milk		Hawaiian Punch
Capri Sun		

Internet and provide 3-D graphics and realistic sounds. In addition to classic Legos, there are Legos that can be programmed via computer to do various tasks. They do not need to buy just walkie-talkies, but they can buy complete portable communication and entertainment devices that let users communicate and play with one another via infrared rays. Inexpensive digital cameras, downloadable music, DVDs, extreme flavors, and green ketchup are all now being marketed to tweens.

When business people are out of touch with this market, amazing things happen. A few short years ago, a certain toy company persuaded a major investment banker to underwrite its IPO offering, based at least somewhat on the bankers' extremely favorable reaction to a new toy the company planned to market. Sure, the toy was neat. It had a remote control. It was fast and sleek. The problem was this: Kids already were choosing from toys almost exactly like this one. To the toy manufacturer and to the adult bankers, this new item was a lot of fun and very different, but to kids this item already existed. After its successful IPO, this company's new toy item did very poorly. The company wound up firing all its senior managers and came very close to going out of business.

Advertising targeted to today's kids is far from rare. Spending on national television advertising to children reached $1.2 billion in 2002 according to statistics compiled by Initiative Media. Today's tweens view advertising aimed directly to them for items ranging from desserts and dot-coms to toys and travel destinations. Even charities get into the act.

The amount of marketing targeted to today's tweens makes getting their attention a real marketing challenge. A few years ago, kid marketers had the opportunity of offering the first kids product in specific categories. The first frozen food (Kid's Cuisine), the first take-to-school lunch (Lunchables), the first kid-marketed shampoo (L'Oréal for Kids), and so forth. For the most part, these products were rewarded with initial success, brand entrenchment, and lots of excitement. Today, it is not as easy. More than just a few products are designed for kids and advertised and promoted to them.

Nonetheless, there are still great opportunities to market to tweens—as long as you pay attention to what today's tweens will accept. While literally hundreds of products are being manufactured for, and marketed to, kids, it is interesting that at least some categories relevant to tweens have not yet seen kid-marketing efforts. For example, plenty of juice-type drinks are marketed to kids, but what about sodas? What about bottled waters? There are plenty of frozen ice cream novelties, but what about ice cream in general? Canned fruits and vegetables, fresh fruits and vegetables, and paper products? At best, there is only a minimal effort. Many of today's tweens have their own bathrooms, but where are the bathroom tissues, toilet tissues, and bar soaps they might want?

Even with the amount of advertising that is targeted to kids today, there are still ways to reach this target group with well-placed ad messages. We'll have more to say about that later.

CONCLUSIONS

Tweens are an extremely profitable consumer segment. The size, spending power, needs, and targetability of this group presents a serious financial opportunity to today's marketers. It is highly advisable to pre-screen product concepts, advertising, and other marketing efforts with tweens before actually launching into the marketplace.

To be successful, marketers involved with the tween segment should take pains to continually keep up with the rapidly changing trends and attitudes of today's tweens as well as the rapidly changing marketplace itself.

3

WHAT DRIVES TWEENS?

Recently, one of our 8-year-old sons received a Christmas gift from his grandmother. It was a bright red fleece sweatshirt with a high-front-zipper collar. Initially he was very excited about it. It was very in-style from his perspective and just his size. Then he noticed something on the sweatshirt—a small, red heart sewn on the top right front as a brand emblem from the manufacturer. He looked over at his younger (age 6) brother's blue sweatshirt that also had an emblem sewn on the front pocket, but that emblem said U.S.A.

Our 8-year-old son turned to us and simply said, "I'll take the blue sweatshirt." Because the blue sweatshirt already was a gift to his brother, switching the shirts was not an option that would have gone over very easily. So he suggested that we go trade it in for another color. When we asked, "Why don't you like the red sweatshirt? You like your other red clothes," he simply said that he didn't like this red and wanted another color, all the while staring directly from the heart logo to the U.S.A. logo on the other sweatshirt.

Why didn't he want to keep the red sweatshirt that he initially liked so much? The answer is all part of the complex psychological make-up of what drives or motivates the actions and attitudes of today's tweens.

Before we delve much further into the motivational drivers of tweens, we want to make sure that our readers understand that we are not psychologists, social behaviorists, or child development experts by any means. However, we have worked side by side with these experts and many others in our years of researching and developing marketing programs for this age group. A team of professionals within our company, WonderGroup, developed the information we present in this chapter. It serves here as a template for deductive understanding of tween emotional "drivers."

Now back to the red sweatshirt. What was the issue with the red heart emblem? It wasn't that he doesn't like hearts, or that he didn't like the color red. It was that he didn't want to be seen by his friends, and older schoolmates, wearing something that might be interpreted as a girl's sweatshirt. On the surface, this seems straightforward and easily understood. We have heard for many years that "boys will be boys, and girls will be boys, but boys won't be girls." In other words, many girls will wear a sweatshirt that is clearly made for a girl or a boy, but a boy will not wear clothing specifically made for a girl. His reaction could be explained simply by the fact that girls and boys are different. However, you can more easily interpret it once you understand how beliefs influence and drive a tween's behavior.

Tween boys and girls are in the midst of some of the most fundamental changes they will go through as people, as discussed in Chapter 1 regarding physical and social changes. In this chapter we will dig deeper and look at the emotional state of tweens.

Younger children have an incredibly strong dependence on adults and yet continually test the boundaries of parental limits and reactions. When these same kids reach their teen years, there is a force just as incredibly strong towards independence that is usually identified with parental separation and personal isolation into their own worlds (bedroom, friends, and so forth).

However, during those years between being a young kid and being a teenager, physical changes and emotional changes are complicated and a challenge for both tweens and their parents. It is common for tweens to show affection towards their parents one minute and to announce a few hours later that they no longer want to be part of the family or that everybody hates them. This sometimes-volatile emotional state is expressed as highs and lows. It can be driven by tween issues such as personal relationships, school violence, and family separations, or by what seems like relatively benign issues such as it being time to turn off the Game-Boy and come to dinner.

It is also a time when not everything is in harmony when it comes to development. Cognitively and physically today's tweens are developing faster than ever. They are acquiring critical thinking skills and huge amounts of information in elementary school and on the Internet. Physically they are reaching sexual maturity at an earlier age than did their parents. Yet emotionally, tween development has not kept up. Tweens today are under more pressure than their parents were to understand how to relate to family, peers, the opposite sex, and themselves.

In order to understand what motivates and drives tweens' interest in products or services, we need to gain a better understanding of the psychological framework that drives behavior. Abraham Maslow (1908–1970), known as a leading advocate of humanistic psychology, developed and published his theory regarding human development that has become known as "Maslow's Hierarchy of Needs." Maslow's theory, usually graphically portrayed as a pyramid (Figure 3.1), hypothesizes that there are five stages to human motivation, and that a person moves through the hierarchy of needs by satisfying the lower-order needs before being motivated by higher-order needs.

The most basic stage—the one that motivates base behavior—is *Physiological Needs*. These needs include food, water, shelter, and the physical necessities for survival. Tweens have relied on parents or guardians for the fulfillment of their physiological needs since they were children, and they assume without much thought that these needs will continue to be met by adults. However, during the tween years they begin to understand the bigger world and take more notice of real-life situations such as homelessness, crime, starvation, and losses associated with natural disasters. This awareness helps lead this age group to more involvement in social causes.

FIGURE 3.1

Maslow's Hierarchy of Needs

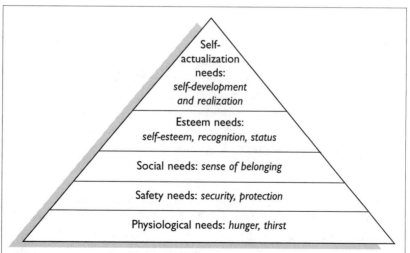

The second level of Maslow's hierarchy is *Security Needs.* This stage involves the base motivational behavior of self-preservation. Tweens, as do all youth segments, see themselves as invincible.

Tweens have moved past the stage of younger kids when separation from an adult resulted in an immediate fear of the unknown, to a more clear understanding that there are consequences to actions, some of which may be harmful. Tweens are also more aware of actions that can be harmful to others, as shown in the first pages of this book where the girl convinced her father to stop smoking. Security needs move from being parent-managed to parent-tween managed. For instance, many tweens have beepers so their parents can keep in touch with their children, even when they are just at a friend's house. (These beepers have also become communication tools that tweens use to keep in touch with each other, especially in split families where the tween moves between mom's house and dad's house on a changing schedule.) Today, about 16 percent of all tweens even have cell-phones, according to a year 2002 NeoPets study, primarily to be able to contact their parents whenever they need them. This number has changed dramatically from the publication of our first edition, which cited that 5 percent of tweens claimed ownership of cell-phones in 1999.

The third and fourth stages of Maslow's hierarchy are *Social Needs* and *Ego or Esteem Needs.* We will go into these motivational stages in greater depth in the next few pages, so we will just mention them here. Social Needs are most often defined as a sense of belonging. In many ways, the tween years are the critical stage in life where boys and girls begin to move outside of a very small social circle. Friendships bloom and change over this period; tweens join sports teams, move to social interest groups such as scouts, and start seeking a personal understanding of where they fit-in, and where they don't.

Esteem needs are personal, or inwardly defined, perspectives about one's self—an understanding of one's self-esteem and the esteem of others. When talking about youth segments, people often mention teenagers and their ego needs. However, even tweens are keenly aware of how they feel, usually in relation to someone else or a group of their fellow tweens. How to interpret feelings, when to show or not show feelings, and identification of personal accomplishment, all weigh heavily on tweens' minds.

Maslow's final stage of his hierarchy of needs is the pinnacle of human achievement, *Self-Actualization Needs.* This level constitutes the personal self-fulfillment of all human needs. Because we don't know of any self-actualized adults, we make the assumption that there are no self-actualized tweens, either. However, given the drive and intelligence of today's tweens, they may have a better shot at getting there than did our generation.

Tweens emerge from the younger-child stage knowing that family or parental guardians will satisfy most of their physiological and security needs. They have also developed the ability for complex and logical thought processes. This leads to a stage in their lives where they begin to seek the satisfaction of higher-order needs. They begin to identify and act upon their own beliefs in order to achieve levels of satisfaction for both social needs and ego needs.

BEHAVIORAL MOTIVATORS

The personal beliefs of tweens that drive most of their behaviors usually can be traced back to one of two things: social needs, wants, and desires, and personal (ego) needs, wants, and desires.

Social Needs, Wants, and Desires

A tween's social life moves from being involved with a close-knit community of family and friends to a much larger social set of acquaintances. Complete immersion into elementary school usually triggers this evolution. Most 8 year olds spend the equivalent of an adult's 40-hour work week at school (including travel time). A large number of tweens today have been acclimated even earlier to this type of environment by attending preschool or daycare programs. According to the National Center for Education Statistics, more than 3.3 million children (56 percent) aged 3 to 5 are in nursery school programs.

The words *social acceptance* are often a catchall term for many forms of behavioral motivation by tweens. When Ashley, who is 10, gets ready for a slumber party, she makes certain decisions based upon the premise of being "socially accepted" at the party. She also makes other decisions to be sure she is not embarrassed or singled-out in a negative way.

Ashley carefully goes through her closet and dresser drawers to pick out the clothes and pajamas that will be seen as "cool" by her friends. She picks out fun clothes and pajamas that she got from Limited Too, her favorite store and the favorite store of many of her friends. She also puts her three favorite flavors of Bonne Bell Lip Smackers in her overnight bag; again, something she knows her friends will like. Ashley is exhibiting motivational behavior driven by social beliefs. She wants to make her choices and behavior conform to what she thinks will reflect on her positively in this social situation.

Ashley sleeps with eight stuffed animals on her bed each night; her favorite is a black and white Panda bear she has named Pandy. She makes sure that Pandy is on her bed every night before going to sleep. Before going to her friend's sleepover, however, Ashley contemplates taking Pandy and makes a conscious decision to leave the stuffed animal in her room. She is concerned that she might be the only one to bring a stuffed animal and one of her friends might make fun of her. This is also an example of motivational behavior driven by her social beliefs. Ashley does not want to risk being singled out as the one who is still childish.

Personal (Ego) Needs, Wants, and Desires

Who am I? How am I the same as or different from my parents? What do I believe? How do I want to act? What makes me feel good? Tweens are grappling with the fact that they are indeed growing up—that they have a defined place in the world. The tween years are when they begin to deal with themselves emotionally in the context of the world that surrounds them. Tweens deal with triumphs of achievement and the struggles of having feelings hurt by things peers say and think about them.

Girls are more attuned to a sense of beauty and appearance. They have picked up cues from adults and teens about the importance of looking good and that feeling pretty is personally satisfying. While boys at this age do not concentrate on personal appearance as much as girls, they also are acutely aware of how they look.

In many communities today, early childhood sports teams include both boys and girls on the same team. T-ball teams and instructional soccer are good examples. However, starting with the tween years, most communities separate the sexes into girls' leagues and boys' leagues. Boys and girls leave an era of childhood in which participation in sports for fun evolves into personal accomplishments and competition.

Tweens are still much attuned, and for some choices subservient, to the choices and directives of their parents.

It is always wise to remember that parents can applaud, approve, accept, tolerate, disapprove, veto, and negate decisions made by the tween. While there is a strong personal belief set within the tweens themselves that drives decisions, they are still much attuned, and for some choices subservient, to the choices and directives of their parents. In Ashley's case, her mother could have told her not to take her Lip Smackers to the sleepover. Even if she was motivated to argue her point of view, her mother's authority would probably carry the day and the Lip Smackers would have remained at home.

MOTIVATIONAL PLATFORM "DRIVERS"

Now that we are familiar with tween social and ego needs, we can delve deeper and identify the specific motivational platforms, or "drivers" that underscore particular choices by tweens.

There are four essential motivators for today's tweens: power, freedom, fun, and belonging. Each of these broad platforms has both social and personal implications for tweens.

Power

Power, as we will discuss later in this chapter, is basically about control and the ability to participate in, or make decisions for one's self and one's social set. For a tween, power indicates the ability to control a situation, someone, or something. There are many great examples of movies and commercials in which tweens outwit adults—a clear portrayal of power.

Freedom

Freedom or independence is complicated in that tweens are exploring these issues and look to teens for some indicators of how to be independent, but they also relish the protective umbrella provided by their family. In general, the tween-age is the age where kids begin to want to "fly" from the nest and become free of their parents' demands. This becomes an ever increasing driver as they become older transitioning tweens (ages 11 to 12). Products like cell phones, pagers, scooters, and the Internet are just some of the items offering our tweens the freedom that they look for.

Products like cell phones, pagers, scooters, and the Internet are just some of the items offering our tweens the freedom that they look for.

Fun

If you ask a tween how to define fun, the usual response is "it's just fun." Fun seems to be a state of mind and activity that has to do with anything other than work, sadness, or fear. In most instances, an element of fun is a given motivational behavior for tweens. While younger children are likely to enjoy the simpler fun-play offered by such items as animal-shaped foods and basic toys, tween fun is also likely to come from more thought-provoking fun situations like grossing out adults, word games, and puns.

Belonging

The final of the four broad motivational forces, belonging is possibly the force that is most attuned to the tween segment as a whole. Again, there are both personal and social implications, but the importance of acceptance by the group is the utmost concern of most tweens. It is played out everyday in classrooms, on playgrounds, and in neighborhoods.

To obtain a better understanding of the strength of this driver, we recently subjected dozens of tween girls to four image boards (see Figure 3.2), each of which depicted one of the four basic drivers: power, freedom, fun, and belonging. We asked each of the tweens to tell us which of these boards best explained how they see themselves. The winner? More chose the board depicting belonging than any other choice. You can begin to understand better why the Internet has become such an important tool for today's tweens. It allows tweens to communicate with others, read gossip, and scan other online information to find out what will be in or out. In second place was the board depicting fun.

Belonging also encompasses many elements; one of the most easily recognized is friendship. Friendships are many and change often during tween years. Tween friendships are social and full of play, laughing, and giggling. Older teenage friendships begin to take on a stronger bonding structure and become more restricted and intimate. While tweens will often say they have many best friends, teens will usually say they have one or two best friends.

This discussion leads us to ask what elements of human behavior comprise these social and personal motivational platforms we call fun, freedom, power, and belonging. We have identified a number of individual "core drivers" that motivate tween behavior, and we call them centrics.

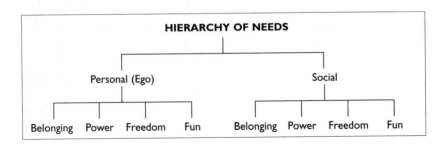

FIGURE 3.2
Personal Motivational Platforms

Power: *Indicates the ability to control a situation, someone, or something.*

(continued)

FIGURE 3.2
Continued

Belonging: *This is the most important need for tween girls.*

FIGURE 3.2
Continued

Fun: *This is the second most important need.*

(continued)

FIGURE 3.2
Continued

Freedom: *Tweens begin to want to "fly" from the nest.*

TWEEN CENTRICS

We define *centrics* as the core drivers that motivate the behavior of tweens. Many of these same centrics can be applied to other age segments. However, the relationship between these centrics and the needs, wants, and desires of tweens provides insights that can be applied to products, services, or communications that will speak directly to tween audiences.

Why should marketers look this deeply into motivational forces? It's because tweens are adept at identifying whether you are sincere or simply trying to appease them. Tweens are very detail-oriented and will readily identify with you if you have accurately identified your product or service with their motivational drivers.

On the other hand, tweens can just as easily give you the cold shoulder if they determine that you are not genuine, or if you are not connecting with them. Many times, we have seen companies that tell us their

FIGURE 3.3
Centrics

FACTORS THAT DRIVE TWEEN BEHAVIORS		
Need	**Motivational Platform**	**Selected Centric**
Personal	Belonging	Worth
		Familiarity
	Power	Mastery
		Intelligence
		Rebellion
	Freedom	Individuality
		Uniqueness
		Independence
	Fun	Imagination
		Simplicity
		Sensation
Social	Belonging	Popularity
		Friendship
		Assimilation
	Power	Superiority
		Control
		Love
	Freedom	Imitation
		Exploration
	Fun	Amusement
		Creativity

target is the tween segment, but they acquire a license partner or apply a licensed property to their product that skews too young. Then they wonder why the product is not jumping off the shelves. Just ask any tween. They will immediately identify that the product is not for them, and the reasoning can be traced back to tween centrics that can be applied to the belonging driver platform.

We identify tween centrics for marketing purposes to fuel product development, marketing, and promotion advertising efforts. These insights then allow retailers, manufacturers, or distributors to create and market their products in a manner that drives trial and purchase activity.

We will discuss in greater detail a few of the tween centrics we have identified. These may help you evaluate insights you have gained and apply them to tween initiatives for your products or services.

Worth

The tween centric of worth is a core driver that motivates both positive and negative behavior. Tweens evaluate their worth based upon a number of internal and external forces. Actions and behavior are molded as a result of reinforcement of this measure of self-esteem. For years, writings by social behavior experts have extolled the fact that conditioning of personal worth takes place in the adolescent years. Tweens who are repeatedly given negative messages by parents, other adults, or peers that they are "a bad seed" or "not smart" or "not good enough" will be left with challenges to their self-worth that may easily extend into their adult years. On the other hand, tweens who are praised for personal achievement and positive behavior, and offered constructive processes for improvement, develop positive self-worth.

Several cosmetic companies have combined style and fashion products for this market with packaging and advertising communications based upon the worth centric.

What does it mean for marketers? Many companies created long-lasting brand impact by providing products, services, and communications that support aspects of positive self-worth and are therefore readily accepted by tweens. For example, several cosmetic companies have combined style and fashion products for this market with packaging and advertising communications based upon the worth centric. A number of companies have also constructed parts of their Web site communications programs to allow tweens to send feedback to the company, to post messages, and, in some instances, to post ideas and artwork. All of this reinforces the importance and value of tweens to the companies that own their favorite brands. Messages such as "you are important" and "you can make a difference" are derived from this centric. L'Oréal has tapped into it to become the leading shampoo for the younger set. The company's internal directive to develop the product with kids in mind has led to packaging that is unique and fun, with colors and scents that are specifically appealing to tweens. Tweens get the message that the shampoo is made "just for us" by L'Oréal, a company that obviously cares about us. The advertising theme, "Because we're worth it, too," really drives this centric-based message home.

Mastery

The *American Heritage Dictionary* defines *mastery* as "possession of consummate skill." Mastery is the base motivational driver for achievement, excelling at an endeavor, and proficiency to the point of personal acceptance and even enjoyment. The tween years are filled with mastery, education, and realization. The years spent in elementary and middle school are about learning and applying new knowledge. The educational process teaches tweens such skills as reading, applied mathematics, and logical thinking, as well as an appreciation of sports and exercise, music and art.

Some tweens easily master some athletic or knowledge-based skills for which peers and adults recognize them. Others decide by themselves, or through social pressure, that they do not or cannot achieve the mastery of some things, and they tend to avoid these pursuits.

Tweens, girls and boys, say such things as the following:

- "I'm not very good at sports."
- "I can read much better than everyone else in my class."
- "I'm a very fast runner."
- "I don't like math."
- "I got all my spelling words correct."
- "I built the entire thing by myself."

All these statements are based upon the centric of mastery and the personal achievement of mastery skills for oneself and in comparison with peers.

What does it mean for marketers? Gatorade, Nike, Reebok, and other brands have tapped into this tween centric for product positioning and communications with tweens. Reebok, recognizing the inherent strength of this centric for tween boys, created a shoe that allows the wearers to measure how high or far they jump, how fast they run, and even provides for gaming such as freeze-tag. The shoes, called Reebok Traxtar, accomplish this with a built-in technology chip. Traxtar's advertising campaign included broadcast and print advertisements.

Ads in *Sports Illustrated for Kids, Nickelodeon,* and *Disney Adventures* featured the headline: "At this instant, you are hurling through the universe. You don't need a shoe that keeps up. You need one that keeps score."

More than a half million tweens were wearing Traxtars within the first full year of product release, providing countless possibilities for monitoring personal mastery.

Individuality

Individuality as a tween centric is somewhat complicated. On the one hand, it says, "I have my own needs and wants." On the other hand, it says, "I also depend on my parents." Dependence on one's parents is not something that the tween wants to avoid; rather it is something that tweens struggle with in choosing when to pull away and when to embrace their dependence on their parents or guardians. For tweens there is the excitement of beginning to define and establish one's own self, but at the same time a tremendous comfort in knowing that they can quickly move back to the protective umbrella of mom and dad.

A passage from Michael Thompson's book, *Speaking of Boys,* summarized this issue for a woman who asked whether she could regain the status of being "cool" in her son's eyes, a status she enjoyed when he was a younger tween. Thompson's answer to her included the following: "Here is the hard part for parents. Your adolescent son is going to need you for many more years. He needs you to love him, to attend to him, to be present for him. He also needs—and I mean needs in the strongest sense—you to do this for him while he acts as if he doesn't need you. He needs you to do this while he defines what is cool and what is not."

"I'm not a child, and I'm not a teenager."

"I'm not a child, and I'm not a teenager." The rallying cry of tweens is that they want to be heard, noticed, and given recognition as individuals. Most tweens look at older teens and television, movie, and music stars for attitudes, styles, and qualities by which they may aspire to define their individual selves. In most cases, however, these elements of individualism associated with teens are studied but not applied. Most tweens feel very comfortable being a part of the larger tween scene.

The strongest behavior driver associated with the individuality centric is that of choice. The drive to choose one's own clothes, shoes, skateboard, bike color, Lip Smacker flavor, or bedroom-wall color, is tremendously strong. This behavior can be expanded to family influences that take the form of openly lobbying for certain vacation destinations, or the color or model of the new family car.

What does it mean for the marketer? Television commercials produced on behalf of antidrug and antismoking organizations are one of the best examples of communications to this group that use the individuality centric as their base for motivation. Many of these spots feature older tweens who are faced with a dilemma of accepting an offer to use drugs or smoke while facing a fear of not being accepted (the popularity centric). The spots show that when tweens make their own individual decisions not to participate in this activity, they are not shunned, but they are actually accepted by their peers and positively recognized as individuals capable of making their own decisions.

Imagination

Recently we had the opportunity to visit a second grade class. Taped to the wall outside of the classroom were assignments in which the kids wrote about what they would do if they became president of the United States. Writing skills covered the gamut, and spelling in many cases was imaginative, but what really struck us was the thought process involved with many of the answers. Some were straightforward: "I would make good laws." A number were very socially conscious: "I would make laws to help people."

Then there were the interesting ones: "I would do away with school," and, "I would paint the White House red." One of our sons espoused the straightforward philosophy that he would make good laws. Then he added a second mission for his presidency, "I would make flying cars for everyone."

The sense that anything is still possible, along with learning about the realities of our world, makes the tween years exciting, challenging, and intriguing. While tweens are able to sit and talk to an adult about world geogra-

The sense that anything is still possible, along with learning about the realities of our world, makes the tween years exciting, challenging, and intriguing.

phy, they are also able to tell you in detail about the world of magical places where Harry Potter lives. They try to imagine what it is like on the other side of the world (China, for example), but they also enjoy imagining what it would be like to live in another entire world (the world in which an everyday tween like Harry Potter finds out he is really a famous wizard). This is also why cartoons hold such an important place for tweens. They are fun and make believe, but with imagination they can seem almost real.

What does it mean for marketers? By tapping into the tween centric of imagination, many companies have developed products or created marketing campaigns that are extremely appealing to tweens. Entire networks have evolved, such as Nickelodeon and Cartoon Network, that serve as imagination outlets for tweens. Wild Planet has created a line of products designed for the would-be spy. Pillsbury's Toaster Strudels brand offers topping "kits" that allow tweens to create their own breakfast art pieces. Nintendo (GameBoy), Sony (PlayStation), Microsoft (XBOX), and other computer gaming companies offer endless avenues of imaginative challenge. In addition, movie studios have evolved the art of story and imagination into movies that have tremendous appeal to tweens. A few of the highly imaginative movies that have been created and marketed to tweens recently include the Harry Potter series, *Finding Nemo, Monsters, Inc., Master of Disguise, Agent Cody Banks, Shrek, The Lizzie McGuire Movie, Rugrats Go Wild,* and the *Spy Kids* trilogy.

Popularity

Popularity, mentioned earlier in this chapter, is an extremely vital centric to both tween boys and girls. Throughout the tween years, popularity takes on more meaning as individuals begin to assess which social groups they fit into and the ones from which they are excluded. Most tweens, as shown by a number of studies, deem themselves to be popular. That is, they feel widely liked and accepted. In the early tween years, popularity means "liked by a large number of other tweens." By the time the tween reaches age 11 or 12, popularity is a definition. He is popular; she is popular. An 11 or 12 year old can distinguish quickly between who is popular and who is not popular. Being popular begins to take on a social status and being popular within a select in-group can be interpreted as being popular on

In the early tween years, popularity means "liked by a large number of other tweens."

a large scale by other tweens. During the tween years boys also begin to take notice and identify popular girls, and girls do the same with boys.

What does it mean for marketers? Associating your product with the tween centric of popularity can offer strategic direction as well as implications for execution. In many cases, the centric of popularity leads to tween behaviors of mimicking those they consider leaders in style choices and product choices. We have heard in focus groups statements such as, "All the popular kids at school are wearing Candies shoes for dress-up events." In this instance, tween girls have made a strong correlation between Candies and the centric of Popularity. Strategically, one could interpret this insight as, "Popular girls are wearing Candies; therefore if I wear Candies, I will be seen as a popular person." The implication that you will become or maintain your popularity by wearing Candies would be a reasonable and motivating message to this market.

Like all centrics, popularity has both a positive and a negative perspective. Both are equally strong for tweens. For example, the positive range of the popularity tween centric could be personalized as "I am popular." The negative perspective would be interpreted as "I don't want to be unpopular." In some instances, the fear of being associated with the negative range or the drive to avoid it can be a stronger motivator, and possibly more real to the tween, than the promise of achieving popularity.

A brand that has been effective by strategically reinforcing the negative perspective of popularity, albeit targeted primarily to an older audience, is The Gap. Not long ago, they created a campaign that said "everyone is wearing fleece." The implication is that you too should wear a Gap fleece like everyone else, or you might not be "in," or said in another way, "you might be part of the unpopular group."

Friendship

Friendship is one of the most highly regarded centrics of tweens. Friends become increasingly more important during the tween years as social ties outside of the family strengthen. During this stage of development, there is a shift from a state of constant parent participation to parent supervision of friendship groups. Moms or dads take a group of 11 year olds to the movies or to the mall and supervise from a distance. A sleepover is not just one friend but five friends. Play with friends becomes more independent, and the highs and lows of these relationships are a part of growing-up.

For tweens, friendships mainly revolve around having fun with other tweens with whom you like to play and interact.

An important note here is that fun is almost always an inherent subcomponent of tween friendship. Younger kids, even in groups, will have a tendency to play by themselves and interaction is minimal. With teens, friendships become bonding relationships, which can become as significant as family relationships. However, for tweens, friendships mainly revolve around having fun with other tweens with whom you like to play and interact.

What does it mean for marketers? There are a number of companies that have tapped the tween centric of friendship. One of our clients, Toymax, created a product that included a diary, a message communicator, and a privacy lock, and named the product "Girls Best Friend Club." By understanding the tween centric of friendship, we created a television commercial with which tween girls could identify. We played up the fun of sending and receiving secret messages with friends, writing in the journal about things you do with your friends, and locking your room, so your brother can not invade this world you have with your friends. The commercial included fun music and giggling over the secret message that referenced a cute boy in their class. The message tween girls heard was that here is a product that is just for you and your friends, and that we know that friendships are fun and important to you as a tween.

Superiority

Superman is a superior being from another plant who uses his supernatural powers for good and continually triumphs over the forces of evil. Both Angelica and Tommy of *Rugrats* demonstrate their superiority in very different ways. Angelica attempts to dominate and control because she is the oldest. Tommy uses his leadership qualities to organize the gang to accomplish things. Superiority is a centric that can be identified in tweens who have leadership qualities or those who desire these qualities. It is always fun to visit tween classrooms and watch the dynamics that take place regarding leadership. When the teacher asks, "Who wants to lead the class to the lunchroom?" nearly every hand in the classroom stretches out. Leadership skills are learned in both a macro and micro sense during these years. Bring a group of six girls, who are all friends, together in a focus group setting and within minutes it will become clear to the observers who is the leader. The other girls willingly acknowledge the superior standing of the leader and look for cues and acceptance from this individual. In a more macro sense, whole cliques become known as leaders, and the superiority of these groups is known and acknowledged by others.

The drive for importance and personal esteem is an important component of superiority, but in the end, it is the social control that is most recognized by tweens. The fact that as a leader you are held in higher regard by your peers is a strong motivator for this group. In the classic adoption curve developed by Everett Rogers (see Figure 3.4), the tweens who are motivated by the superiority centric are more likely to be early adopters. Innovators (the smallest group) tend to be big risk-takers and thus may be seeking attention, but they do not necessarily embrace leadership. Leaders are usually good at identifying innovation quickly, and they are also good at determining whether to embrace innovation or avoid it based upon social risk. These tweens are more likely to be leaders in fashion, sports, and grades (yes, for this group, intelligence is a leadership quality as opposed to when we were tweens).

Control

From the earliest of ages, children learn through trial and error various methods of controlling situations. As any parent can tell you, kids find inventive ways to control situations to their desired benefit. All of us

FIGURE 3.4
Everett Rogers Adoption Curve

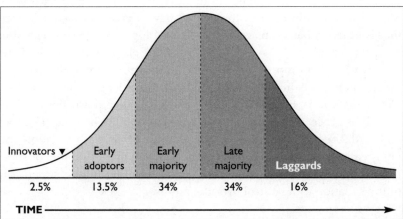

remember numerous instances of standing in a public place as one of our kids threw a tantrum (what parents affectionately call meltdowns) because their parents refused to buy something they wanted. Somewhere along the line as a parent, you find that you pick your battles. Sometimes you hold your line, and sometimes you buy them the piece of candy they want so you can maintain your sanity. When kids move to the tween years, these out-of-control tantrums are replaced by sheer persistence, the art of negotiation, and other more subtle methods of getting what they want—flowery statements such as "I'll die if I don't get that blouse."

What does it mean for marketers? Marketers have appealed to this tween centric very effectively in recent years. General Mills produced a television campaign in which animated tweens take control of the Fruit Roll-Up factory. WonderGroup helped Heinz determine that a ketchup with a specially designed top that would allow tweens to draw (control) on their food was highly appealing. A green color version of their EZ Squirt Ketchup, which definitely lacks adult appeal, adds another layer of control in that the tween feels a sense of power with a product that is seemingly just for them.

Trolli Gummi Candies, recently acquired by Nabisco, has been effective at tapping into the control centric for the development and marketing of one of its signature offerings—Sour Brite Crawlers. Trolli recognized that in a category where adults consume most of the products (Gummi Bears, etc.), it would need to be bold in entering the market for tweens. The result of the development efforts was Sour Brite Crawlers, gummi worms that have a bold, sour taste. Not only was the taste much more appealing to tweens than adults, but the format of worms was clearly identified with tween interest in things that have a gross-out factor. In fact, that is exactly what we played-up in Trolli's highly successful television campaign. A couple of tween boys are in an elevator with their skateboards when a group of adults in business attire comes aboard. The tweens then talk behind the backs of the adults at length about how they like to eat worms, bite them in half, and suck them down slowly, while the adults proceed to become sick from what they are hearing. The spot ends with the adults running off the elevator while the boys laugh and enjoy eating their Sour Brite Crawlers. This is a great example of superiority in the macro sense, where tweens demonstrate their superiority of the situation with control over the adults.

Imitation

There is an important difference between what you might assume tweens are doing and what they are actually doing.

When we began to develop a deeper understanding of the behavioral motivators of tweens, we often talked about aspiration. However, it is not in the list of centrics because we have found, through our continuing study of youth segments, that there is an important difference between what you might assume tweens are doing and what they are actually doing.

We used to talk a lot about tweens aspiring to be stars like Britney Spears, or Justin Timberlake, or older teens. This aspirational force, we initially concluded, was what drove them to dress like these role models, to assume attitudes like these role models, and to be stars alongside of them. Instead, what we have deduced, is that tweens in fact are very comfortable being tweens and in most cases do not want to be teens yet, and they really don't want to be Britney or Christina. What they really want to be is part of the social throng of fans, or an in-style kid. Instead of aspiration, mimicking or imitation drives the centric they are expressing. A tween can comfortably imitate these role models to the point of looking and acting like them, with freedom to have fun as opposed to the pressure of achievement associated with aspiration.

What does it mean for marketers? Some companies have been very successful at identifying tween stars early and then incorporating them or their style in products, promotions, and communications. Recently, there has been a surge of musicians who have incredible appeal to tweens. At least some of the appeal comes from marketing aimed directly at the tween segment by the music labels of rising stars.

Amusement

We had a New Year's Eve party with a couple of our friends and their families. Most of the kids ranged in age between second and fifth grade. At one point, we had not heard from the kids in a while so we went down to the basement to see what they were all up too. We were amazed to see that every kid (nine in all) had some form of a toy sword, light saber, pirate blade, etc., in one hand and a protective shield in the other. The kids were all playing sword fighting, and I even heard them talking to each other about not hitting too hard. The most amazing thing of all was

Tweens have a strong sense of fun, and a social group can quickly turn into organized chaos.

that right in the middle of this group along with the 7-year-old to 9-year-old boys were three 10-year-old to 11-year-old girls. We asked what everyone was doing, and the chorus of response was, "We're just playing." This is a perfect example of the strong behavioral motivator of fun or amusement as it pertains to a social setting. Tweens have a strong sense of fun, and a social group can quickly turn into organized chaos. It should be noted that a strong peer leader can negate certain social play activities (i.e., "Let's not play that," or "That sounds stupid.") or rally the troops quickly. In some instances the will of the group can even override a leader opposed to the activity. ("OK, I've decided to play, too.")

What does it mean for marketers? With its campaign to reinstate "Family Game Night," Hasbro has done an excellent job of connecting with both tweens and their parents. A resurgence of interest in board games generally, along with Hasbro's campaign centered on social fun in a family setting, has proven to be a win-win for their board games unit (Milton Bradley and Parker Brothers).

MULTIPLE CENTRICS

Although we have provided a detailed look at only a few of the tween centrics, you can explore the others in the same manner. In application, note that these centrics can be mixed and melded based upon the category, the product, the message, and the consumer insight. For example, when we talked about the Reebok Traxtar shoes, we noted that it touched on the tween centric of mastery. The shoes also have affiliation with other tween centrics including

- *popularity* (as they become a trend or "must have" product on the playground);
- *superiority* (I have Traxtars and you don't); and
- *amusement* (they have social games such as freeze-tag in their programmed audio chip).

In some cases you may need to evaluate the consumer insights, uncover the pertinent motivational platforms, review your competition's positioning, and then make a decision about the most motivating foundation for your product or advertising.

ADDITIONAL CENTRICS

Following are examples of other centrics that you may want to investigate and include in your marketing strategy development process:

- *Familiarity* (Personal—Belonging) Stability is important and there is a comfort in things a tween knows. There may be hesitancy with new or unfamiliar things, especially if there is a risk of embarrassment.
- *Intelligence* (Personal—Power) Most tweens feel they are smart people and like being perceived as smart by peers and adults.
- *Rebellion* (Personal—Power) Tweens, as they age, seek to establish separation from parental control, usually manifested through benign rebellious behavior and acts.
- *Uniqueness* (Personal—Freedom) The desire to feel special as identified by a personal trait, activity, or action.
- *Independence* (Personal—Freedom) Tweens exhibit a growing desire for the responsibility associated with self-reliance, as individuals and within groups.
- *Simplicity* (Personal—Fun) Tweens do not enjoy dealing with subjects or issues that are too complicated, such as a product that is very difficult to build or use. The easier something is to understand, the more likely tweens will regard it as fun.
- *Sensation* (Personal—Fun) Appeal to the unique senses of tweens has been successful for many companies as evidenced by taste sensations such as super sour, the visual sensations of colored ketchup and light-up gel yo-yo's, to physical sensations such as crackling candy (Crazy Dips).
- *Assimilation* (Social—Belonging) A tween belongs to an entire social set of peers their age, differentiated from teens, adults, and younger children.
- *Love* (Social—Power) This is the concept of an unspoken bond of loyalty and caring for and by family, pets, and even teddy bears and music stars.
- *Exploration* (Social—Freedom) Tweens have a strong desire to learn, experience and begin pushing the boundaries of the world they live in, from their physical environment to the emotional beginnings of attraction to the opposite sex.
- *Creativity* (Social—Fun) There is a joy in humor, jokes and puns, inventions and games, and the ability to think about things without adult parameters. Almost anything is possible.

A FEW IMPLICATIONS

- Tweens are complicated emotional beings. Do your homework carefully and thoroughly. Uncover the centrics that drive behavior. Dig deeper than cursory methodologies. Use tween-focused research and insight-gathering techniques, and complement these with observation. Then test to validate your findings.

- The basic need to fit in with, and belong to, their group of peers has tremendous significance to marketers of "billboard" type products—products that tweens must use in public. If a tween must use your product in front of friends, she is likely to need some assurance that your product would not make her seem "uncool" or too young. Therefore, marketers of billboard-type products might need to take steps to help tweens learn about their products. Make sure of tween acceptance ahead of time. This is especially true for fashion items. Advertising must be in the "right" vehicles and on the right Web sites.

- Marketers of tween products must minimize the possibility of having their products appear to be for younger kids. Packaging must not look to babyish. Talent pictured in ads or on the package must be tweenage or older.

- Qualitative market research must be careful to notice and minimize peer-pressure bias. Peer pressure in tween focus groups is a huge danger. In fact, our own experience has found that what tweens say in groups and what they say or do in private can be dramatically different. For example, in listening to tween girls aged 8 to 10, one would think that they have totally stopped playing with dolls. Yet, visit a bedroom, and surprise!

- Consider the importance of peers throughout much of the marketing mix. Advertisers would be wise to show tweens in groups. Promotions could foster club/group/friend participation.

- Younger tweens have not yet left the family. They still rely heavily on mom's approval. Retailers of items designed for the young tween must make it inviting for tweens, especially girls, to shop with their moms. Advertisers may, in some cases, be wise to reinforce to this audience that "moms will approve of it too."

4

TWEEN MONEY AND INFLUENCE

Because tweens still depend heavily on parent spending and money, their true power lies not in their purchasing power, but in the ability to influence their parents (and grandparents) to make purchases on their behalf.

In fact, tweens are the most *influential* youth market group of all for the following reasons:

- *Unlike younger children,* tweens are better information processors and can better understand and communicate exactly what they want—including specific brand names. Figure 4.1 shows that as kids grow to be tweens, parents are far less likely to be the sole decision-makers for tween-related items.
- *Unlike younger children,* parents actually rely more on tweens to help them around the house in many ways. This includes asking them to help make purchase decisions and even shopping lists.
- *Unlike teens,* tweens are more reliant on others' money and must rely on influence to secure the products they want and need.
- *And, unlike teens,* whose influence and concerns shift towards bigger ticket items, tweens are still very involved with many day-to-day, lower-cost items, such as what goes into their lunch boxes, or what is in the house for afternoon snacks.

FIGURE 4.1
Tween Impact on Purchases

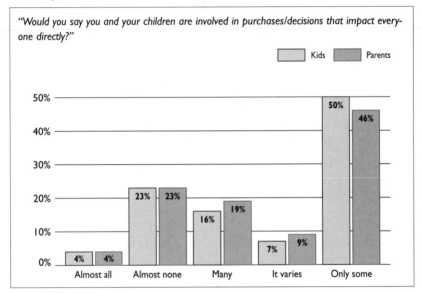

"Would you say you and your children are involved in purchases/decisions that impact everyone directly?"

Source: Roper Youth Study: February 2003

Parents relinquish more decisions to kids as they grow older. It is assumed that tweens capture more of the decision making through influence, while teens capture more by actually making purchases themselves.

TWEENS ARE "HIDDEN" PERSUADERS/INFLUENCERS

Many marketers are finally becoming savvy to kid influence, but most marketers well underestimate it. In hundreds of focus groups and concept tests we have conducted over the past few years, we have found that much of the true power of today's tween influence is often far from obvious to parents or to marketers.

Let's take a closer look at the many, often hidden, factors affecting the way in which today's tweens influence household decision making.

The Training Factor

Tweens train their parents without the parents knowing it. Once parents have purchased an item for their tween as a result of being influenced, they are likely to repurchase that item again and again without the need for (or awareness of) any additional influence. Specifically, in recent focus groups, moms told us that they limited their kids to only three requests per shopping trip. However, their tweens later told us (in subsequent focus groups) that they trained their moms to know what to buy for them during previous shopping trips. Therefore, during upcoming shopping trips they would now request new items they had not asked for before. (Smart!)

The Habit Factor

Today's parents do not realize that it has become a habit to ask their tweens continually to influence them. In parent groups, moms often say that after a busy day at work, or just before going shopping, they'll ask their kids what they should bring home from the store or, more times than not, "Where do you want to go to eat?"

The Hidden Message Factor

Additionally, parents have even unknowingly been influenced to see various advertising that, in turn, leads to future product purchases. How many parents regularly ask their kids, "What do you want to watch on TV tonight?" Other times, they just join their tweens in viewing a show that is already tuned in. After busy workdays, hassle-free time with their kids is an important part of the day. To avoid hassles, many parents would rather just watch the programs that their kids want to watch.

FIGURE 4.2
Share Gained by Nagging

"Would not have purchased the product if not nagged."	
Place-based Entertainment	41%
Quick Service Restaurants	33
Movies	32
Apparel	31
Home Video	30
Theme Parks	21
CD-Roms	33
Food	34
Toys	46
Snacks	40
Cereals	39
Beverages	24

Source: The Nag Study, Western Media

Beware of the Danger of No-Influence!

By far, the biggest mistake that we have seen marketers make is not understanding what can happen if a tween does not ask for an item. In trying to keep their lives as simple as possible, parents will often *not* buy an item, unless their child actively asks them to buy it (see Figure 4.2). This will occur even when parents think that their child would like the item. The fact is, today's moms do not want to risk the time or the money to bring home items that their kids may not eat or drink.

The 2003 Yankelovich Youth MONITOR reveals that a high percentage of mothers consider their child's preference very or somewhat important in a wide range of categories, from clothing to breakfast cereals. (See Figure 4.3.)

The Nag Factor Study, conducted in 1997–1998 by Initiative Media (formerly Western Media), found that, on average, sales volume of items purchased for kids declined by one-third if kids did not ask for them.

Just think what this could mean in trying to read new product concept tests? It seems that when evaluating new product concepts and determining whether moms will purchase an item for their kids, moms actually score the concept with the assumption that their kids will ask them for the item. If, in fact, the marketer does not intend to advertise its new item to the tween, the chance of mom being asked for the item is virtually nil. The result? Possibly high concept test score, but in reality, no asking, no purchase!

> *Parents tend to score a new product concept with the assumption that their kids would ask for it*

We observed an indication that parents tend to score a new product concept with the assumption that their kids would ask for it in a recently completed concept test for one of our food clients. We tested a very interesting new kids' food concept among moms and tweens. Both the moms and the tweens gave the new concept an A+, ranking this concept among the top 5 percent of all new product concepts rated by this particular testing service. On a hunch, we then asked the moms what their opinion of the concept would be if their kids did not ask them for the item. The result? Mom's opinion of the item dropped from A+ to a B.

As a further example, several years ago when Power Rangers was still a top television program, we had an opportunity to helping a client launch Power Ranger Cheese—an item that when concept tested among moms did extremely well. In fact, the concept scored so highly among moms that we made the mistake of telling the client not to advertise the product to kids. After all, moms told us that they would definitely buy Power Ranger Cheese because they already knew that their kids would love it.

Power Ranger Cheese bombed! Why? Follow-up research found that, among

FIGURE 4.3
Factors Influencing Parents when Buying Food for Children

When buying food for children, kids' influence is far more important than advertising.	
Price	62%
Child request	57
Good taste	44
Coupons	38
Ads	6

Source: Mark Clements Research, 1995

other reasons, moms elected not to buy the product once in the marketplace because their kids did not ask them for it—they couldn't because they had not seen advertising. When kids did not ask their moms to buy Power Ranger Cheese, they bought their typical brand instead. After all, they knew that their husbands liked Kraft, and because their kids didn't ask for anything else, well, why waste the money?

Perhaps the next biggest mistake marketers make is failing to realize what can happen to a seemingly poor new product idea when a tween *actively* asks for it. Here, too, we have seen companies go to great lengths to come up with some neat new kid concepts and then test these ideas not with kids, but with their parents! In too many cases, we observed companies ready to walk away from an idea because moms voiced disapproval during focus groups. However, when we ask the same nonapproving moms what they would do "if their child asked them to buy the item," guess what? They usually said they would go ahead and try it anyway.

The Veto Factor

Negative influence is even worse. Another tween force just as powerful as influence on the success or purchase of many household items is negative influence.

Marketers know that kids and tweens are highly influential in getting their parents to go to McDonald's, Burger King, and Pizza Hut. However, they may not realize that tweens can be a significantly negative force involving other restaurants if those restaurants do not have the food, atmosphere or fun that they want.

Tweens are especially capable of getting their parents *not* to buy or use items even when parents know that these items will be good for their kids. Although their products can be life enhancing to kids, marketers of health and nutrition products, safety and medical devices, and even pharmaceuticals may not be successful if kids are against using them. In just about every focus group that we have ever conducted concerning health-oriented food products for kids, we have moms say that unless their kids think it is cool, made for them, and so forth, forget about it.

The incidence of asthma among tweens today is at an all time high. However, physicians tell us that while kids today are using their inhalers, doctors rarely even try to get them to use an extension piece that would make the inhalers more effective. Why? Because the extensions are

Marketers of health and nutrition products and even pharmaceuticals may not be successful if kids are against using them.

too big and kids think they are ugly. Why not make them telescoping and colorful? Shame on pharmaceutical companies.

If that's not sad enough, one of our own tween daughters is highly allergic to peanuts. She is supposed to carry an Epi Pen wherever she goes, so that she can inject herself and hopefully save her life if she accidentally ingests a peanut. Do you think that we can make her carry around her Epi Pen? No way! It is too big to fit in her purse.

UNDERSTANDING INFLUENCE

The degree to which tweens influence today's purchases is huge. In fact, 80 percent of today's tweens regularly shop for groceries with their parents, according to the July 2003 Harris Interactive YouthPulse. Moreover, the 2003 Yankelovich Youth Monitor study finds that 62 percent of 9 to 11 year olds actually enjoy shopping at the supermarket. We even found that 11 percent of today's tweens report making the family's grocery list. You can bet that when they make these trips or lists, tweens are extremely active in making sure the "right" products make it into the shopping carts.

Our 2003 KidzEyes Internet panel study found that today's tweens strongly affect the purchases of many goods. You can see the magnitude of this influence in Figure 4.4.

HOW IS THIS HAPPENING?

There are other factors involved in the increase of tweens' influence besides their improved nagging skills. Other causal factors are changes in family structure and parenthood, changes in tween income, increased tween responsibilities, and more. Let's look at some of those factors.

Changing Families

Today's tweens live in household structures that greatly encourage, if not depend on, their influence on household purchases.

TWEENS INFLUENCE ON OVERALL SHOPPING

Percent of tweens regularly shopping for groceries	80%
Percent of tweens reporting to enjoy going to supermarket	67
Percent of tweens reporting to make family shopping list	11

Source: Interactive/Nick/MTV Study July 2000

FIGURE 4.4
Tween Purchase Influence

Percent of tweens who usually buy themselves or buy with a parent	
Candy	60%
Games/Toys	57
Books	33
Soft drinks	28
Snacks	27
Jewelry*	42
Nail polish/Perfume*	41
Clothing	18
Computer software	17
School lunch or drinks	15
Fast food	14
Athletic shoes	8
Soap or shampoo	6
*Among girls only	

Source: WonderGroup/Kidzeyes 2003 Study

Moms Working

Many of today's tweens have working moms and dads. In 2002, 62 percent of children living in two-parent households reported both parents working. While this number is actually down versus the last several years, it is still nonetheless a significant majority of kid households.

The Gen X Mom

A primary reason behind the recent drop in the number of working moms is also, oddly enough, a key reason that kids have become more influential in today's families. Today's tween mom is largely a Gen Xer. After growing up as latchkey kids, these Gen Xers prefer to have at least one parent home with their children. But, while she is home, the Gen X mom is far different from her Baby Boom counterpart. Unlike the boomer parent, the Gen Xer encourages her children to become consumers. She actively involves them in purchase decisions, and she actively solicits their opinions! The most recent Yankelovich Youth MONITOR reported that an astounding 78 percent of today's moms actually find it easier to shop when their children know what brands they want her to buy.

Single Parents

PERCENT OF TWO-PARENT HOUSEHOLDS WITH BOTH PARENTS IN THE WORKFORCE	
2002	62%
1999	69
1998	68
1993	66
1988	63

Source: *Current Population Survey*, U.S. Bureau of Labor Statistics

Another big change in the tweens' family structure has been the significant growth in the number of households headed by a single parent. Specifically, in 2002, approximately 1 in 3 children did not live in households with two parents. Almost one-quarter of all children lived with just their moms, 5 percent lived with their dads, and an additional 4 percent lived with neither (see Figure 4.5). Tweens living with single moms are

FIGURE 4.5

Percentage of Children in Household Type (from 2002)

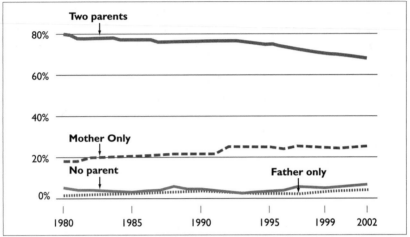

Source: U.S. Census Bureau, March Current Populaton Survey

most likely to have a working mom since almost 8 in 10 single moms work.

Little by little, the number of single-parent households is slowly catching up with the number of households with married parents. Single parents now account for 28 percent of family households with children (Source: Children's Living Arrangements and Characteristics, March 2002).

What is important about this trend is that tweens of single-parent households are even more influential in family purchases than those raised in married-couple homes. In a recent online article, "Growing up in Single Parent Families," the author, Barbara J. Wurzel, states:

> Single parents report differences in parent-child interactions in their new family structure. They see themselves as more respectful and more able to encourage individual opinions from their children. Although they are more likely to report feeling angry toward their children, single parents more often consider the children's preferences.

A study, conducted by Professor Bob Ahuja at Xavier University found that family shopping is three times as common for single-parent households versus families where children have parents who are married.

Most importantly, children of single parents shop alone for the family at three times the rate of children raised in dual parent households.

Home Alone

As kids grow older, the likelihood of them spending time caring for themselves increases. In fact, in 1997, more than 1 in 3 tweens aged 10 to 12 regularly spent at least some time at home alone, and in 2003, our own survey found over 40 percent of tweens aged 10 and older are now home alone at least one day or more a week. Interestingly, while this number is also down somewhat from our 2000 survey—consistent with what we are now seeing among Gen-X households being more "family" oriented (see Figure 4.6).

How does this affect influence? For one thing, kids at home alone understand about what food and supplies the family needs. Either they will offer moms suggestions, or mom will ask them what to buy. In addition, perhaps feeling guilty for leaving their kids home alone, moms appear to be more open to their kids' "suggestions."

Parental Attitudes

As previously mentioned, today's Gen-X parents are far more receptive to their children's requests. In fact, they actively solicit their children's help in making purchase decisions. In the 1997–1998 Nag Factor study conducted by Western Media (now Initiative Media), 70 percent of parents were found to be receptive to kid requests. Specifically, four seg-

FIGURE 4.6

Primary Child Care Arrangements of Children with an Employed Parent

	AGE 5	SCHOOL AGE (6 TO 12 YEARS-OLD)
Parent/other care	19%	41%
Before-and-after-school program	8	15
Center-based care	40	—
Family child care	11	7
Nanny/baby-sitter	3	4
Relative care	19	23
Self-care	—	10

Source: The Urban Institute, *1999 National Survey of American Families*

FIGURE 4.7
Parental Receptivity to Kid Nags

INDULGERS (33%)	KIDS PALS (15%)	CONFLICTED (20%)	BARE NECESSITIES (31%)
Pushovers	Child-like	Dislikes kid advertising	Conservative
Impulse Buyers	Enjoys interacting with kids	Don't like kid requests for non-essentials	Purchases are well considered
Indulgent	Kids have significant impact on brand selection	Hard to resist kid requests	Low interaction with their kids
Don't mind kid requests for non-essentials		Kids have significant impact on brand selection	

ments of parents were uncovered: indulgers, kid pals, conflicted, and bare necessities. All but the latter interacted with their kids in purchase decision making (see Figure 4.7).

Their Own Money

Another reason for the significant influence today's tweens have traces back to the money that they themselves now have. Most tweens report earning money from household chores, birthdays, and holidays (see Figure 4.8). In addition, the majority of tweens (56 percent) receive at least some form of allowance from their parents. Older tweens (aged 10 and up) are earning additional funds from activities like babysitting, mowing the lawn, and shoveling snow. Small percentages even report having an after-school job.

Naturally, because of this extra earning power, spending power is significantly greater among older tweens.

HOW MUCH MONEY DO YOU SPEND WEEKLY?		
	8 to 9 year-olds	10 to 12 year-olds
Less than $5.00	76%	61%
More than $5.00	24	39

Source: WonderGroup/KidzEyes 2003 Study

Savings

Not only do today's tweens spend; they save, too. About 60 percent of our KidzEyes Tween panel report that they

FIGURE 4.8

Top Five Ways Tweens Earn Money

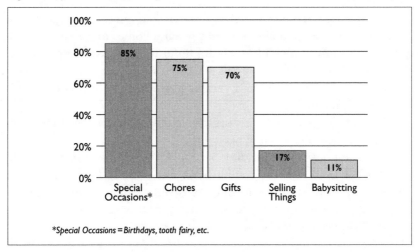

Special Occasions = Birthdays, tooth fairy, etc.

FOR WHAT ARE YOU SAVING?

Boys	Girls
Toys and video games	Vehicle (car)
Vehicles (cars and bikes)	Dolls and CDs

are saving right now to buy something special. What are the top items that they are saving for? The answers varied for boys and girls.

How does increased spending potential affect influence among tweens? Influence is affected in two ways. First, today's parents observe what tweens like to buy for themselves and, therefore, may buy these same items occasionally on behalf of their kids.

Second, we have observed that today's tweens use their money to "strike deals" with their parents. For example, they will "offer" to pay half the cost for more expensive items that they really want, like pagers, cell phones, and clothing.

Purchasing Power

WHAT DO YOU BUY FOR YOURSELF?

Percent Reporting Purchase	
Candy	60
Games/toys	57
Nail polish/perfume (among girls)	41
Books	33
Soda pop	28
Snack food	27
Clothing (transitioning tweens)	25
Clothing (all tweens)	18
Fast food	14

While tweens do not have much spending money of their own, they are, nonetheless, surprisingly active buyers. Tweens report usually or sometimes buying a variety items by themselves.

Total Parent Expenditures

Interestingly, children of both married-couple and single-parent households are treated about equally when it comes to parental spending. Expenditures on children do not differ much among single-parent versus married-couple households. Rather, it seems that expenses of raising a child merely consume a greater percentage of a single-parent's household income.

In a married-couple family with two children, parents will spend on average $9,740 on each child aged 9 to 14.

Average household spending per household is shown in Figure 4.9.

What is especially interesting here is that these figures give us a foundation for the minimum effects of tween influence. Because of this spending, one could say that total influence of tweens, either direct (because of requesting or choosing products) or indirect (through parents "knowing" that their children are requiring certain items) is at least $176 billion. Moreover, this does not count other influential purchases made for the entire family like cars, houses, vacations, etc.

FIGURE 4.9

Average Household Spending per Household

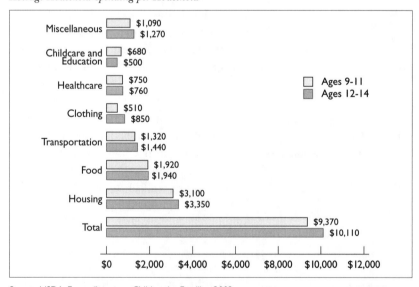

Source: USDA, Expenditures on Children by Families, 2002

AFFECTING INFLUENCE

Many marketers make the mistake of thinking that if tweens are not currently exhibiting strong influence in a category, then that category is not worth marketing to tweens. Wrong! Tweens will influence the purchase of products that they care about. If no product in a specific category appeals specifically to them, then they will exhibit little or no influence. However, if a new product comes along in any category that talks to tweens and appeals to tweens, then watch how their influence in that category grows.

Several years ago, we were helping to launch a new kid-targeted sliced-cheese product. A preliminary look at the cheese category indicated a very low kid influence factor in this category. Our own focus groups confirmed this. Virtually no kid felt that she had any influence in the purchase of the family's cheese. Why? From their point of view, there was no difference between one slice of cheese and another.

When we told these kids about a new type of oversized, sliced cheese (Borden's Big Cheese), these very same kids became highly excited and reported that they would certainly ask their moms' to buy it. Influence was born!

Other product categories suffered from low to no kid influence until a product and marketing effort targeted them. Look at how high the tween influence has become for nail polish and perfume, thanks to Bath & Body Works and Bonne Bell; for jewelry, thanks to Claire's; for school lunches, thanks to Lunchables; yogurts, thanks to Sprink-lins and Go-Gurt.

IMPLICATIONS

- Marketers could make a mistake if they pay attention only to attitudes of parents toward shopping for particular groceries. It is the behavior of the children and the interaction of parents with the children that represent major differences when it comes to various products.
- With the increased responsibilities now placed on tweens, particularly in single-parent families and dual-income families, manufacturers of grocery products might find it fruitful to aim more advertising at tweens.

- When marketing items that are developed for tweens, take steps to make certain that not only parents, but also the tweens themselves, are aware of the product. In the absence of their tweens' request or influence, parents may not buy the items.
- Marketers of kid and tween products with benefits primarily oriented towards moms must do their part in increasing kid desire for the product or moms will not buy or use it. This has special implications for health and nutrition products and supplements as well as even pharmaceutical and medical supply companies.
- Businesses manufacturing family and household products that are used by tweens might want to consider marketing a special tween-oriented product.
- Financial institutions may want to consider tapping into tween savings desires and offer gift savings clubs or tie-ins with music clubs.
- When testing parents' reactions to new kid-product concepts, try to assess the parents' desires for the product in the absence of kid requests. That is, ask parents to assess the product assuming that their child does not know about this product.

5

TWEEN INTERESTS AND ACTIVITIES

The lives of most of today's tweens seem to center on their loves of music (especially among girls) and sports (especially among boys), plus their desire to belong to or fit in with peer groups. A more complete look at the top tween interests reveals some commonalties among the sexes but some key differences as well.

Not surprisingly, musicians and athletes are the "famous" people that today's 8 to 12 year olds would like to meet. Girls go for today's top performers like Avril Lavigne, Eminem, and Britney Spears. Boys want to meet Michael Jordan and Kobe Bryant.

Much of boys' casual talk with friends centers on sports and what to play. Girl tweens, on the other hand, report that their number one topic for talk with friends is guess what? Boys. In addition, because peer acceptance is such an essential driver in this age group, it is not surprising that tween girls report that, when socializing with friends, they love to gossip about other people that they don't like.

TOP TWEEN INTERESTS

Girls 8 to12	Boys 8 to 12
Music	Sports
Nature &	participation
animals	Watching sports
Famous	Nature &
people	animals
Arts & crafts	Music
Fashion	Science
Dance	Famous people

Source: Roper Youth Report 1998

They're Beginning to Feel Busy

It is during the tween years that children seem to begin feeling time pressure. Our 2003 study found about half

79

(48 percent) reporting that they have too much to do everyday (from KidzEyes/WonderGroup study).

Gone are the days when just about all kids got home from school early in the afternoon and ran out to play or watched afternoon cartoons. About one-half of today's tweens go to an after-school program at least once a week, while a little more than one-third go a few days or more. Because of involvement in after-school programs, many of today's tweens do not arrive home until dinnertime. The majority of tweens who participate in after-school activities do not get home until after 5:00 P.M., with almost 30 percent getting home after 6:00 P.M. (see Figure 5.1).

According to KidzEyes April 2003 Kid Power State of the Union study, homework may also play a part in causing kids to feel some time pressure. About 50 percent of today's tweens feel they have too much homework, while 60 percent report having at least one hour of homework daily, and almost 33 percent report having *at least* two hours daily.

Nonetheless, tweens still have other demands on their time when they are not in school or involved in after-school programs.

They Do Chores

One reason tweens seem to be busier today than yesterday and growing up faster than before could lie in their increased responsibility around the house. Our 2003 KidzEyes study found the tween participation in weekly household chores and activities shown at left.

A closer look at tweens' weekly household activities clearly highlights the emerging traditional roles between boys and girls. The largest differences between girl and boy involvement are in washing dishes and doing laundry.

Also, note that 20 percent of tween girls report doing the family shopping list at least once a week—again pointing to the influence tweens have on today's household purchases.

TWEEN PARTICIPATION IN WEEKLY CHORES

Chores/ Activity	Days per Week 1 to 3 days	4 to 7 days
Help clean house	64%	21%
Clean my room	60	25
Help take care of pet	28	44
Shop at a food store	58	4
Set table	42	17
Shop at convenience store	45	4
Wash dishes	32	11
Watch brother/ sister	26	15
Do the laundry	27	4
Shop for family groceries	41	2

Source: WonderGroup/KidzEyes 2003 Study

CHORES DONE AT LEAST ONCE A WEEK

	Boys	Girls	Differ-ence
Clean house	80%	90%	+10
Clean room	84	86	+ 2
Wash dishes	31	56	+25
Make own lunch	51	64	+13
Shop for family groceries	39	46	+ 7
Prepare shopping list	9	20	+11
Make own dinner	23	30	+ 7
Take care of pet	66	77	+11
Laundry	22	36	+14
Prepare family meal	17	30	+13

Source: WonderGroup/KidzEyes 2003 Study

Free-Time Activity

While they are certainly beginning to feel busier, tweens still have ample free time in which to enjoy themselves. According to the 2003 Roper Youth Report, 70 percent of tweens agree that they have enough free time for themselves. Like so many other things in their lives, even tween's use of free time clearly shows this group's desire to fit in with their peers. Almost one-half of both boys and girls report hanging out with their friends to be among their favorite free-time activities. In addition, when asked, the majority of today's tweens report having four or more best friends. Not surprisingly, other favorite free-time activities differ significantly between boys and girls. Boys are more likely to prefer watching television or playing video games and sports, while girls are more likely to read magazines, listen to music, go shopping, or communicate through phone conversations and instant messaging.

FIGURE 5.1
When Tweens Get Home

Question: On days that you have an after-school activity, what time do you usually get home?								
		GENDER		**AGE**		**BOYS**		**GIRLS**
	Total	Boy	Girl	Younger	Older	Younger	Older	Younger	Older
Sample size	224	97	127	87	137	36	61	51	76
Before 2 p.m.	11%	0%	2%	1%	1%	0%	0%	2%	1%
2 to 3 p.m.	0	1	0	0	1	0	2	0	0
3 to 4 p.m.	13	12	13	9	15	6	16	12	15
4 to 5 p.m.	20	22	19	16	23	11	28	20	18
5 to 6 p.m.	37	36	38	37	37	33	38	39	37
6 to 7 p.m.	9	9	9	15	6	22	2	10	9
7 to 8 p.m.	13	12	13	17	10	25	5	12	15
After 8 p.m.	6	7	6	5	7	3	10	6	5

Source: WonderGroup/KidzEyes 2000 Study

FAVORITE FREE-TIME ACTIVITIES	
Hang out with friends	56%
Play sports	55%

Source: Roper Youth Report 1998

Sports

Interestingly, whether it is because of busier schedules, more after-school activities, or greater use of computer/ video games, an analysis of reported tween sports activities by *Sports Illustrated for Kids* reveals a substantial decline in almost every sport played between the years of 1993 and 2000.

Although participation in sports has continued to decline, information from the 2003 Roper Youth Report reinforces the fact that sports are still an important part of life for many tweens. Basketball continues to be the number one sports activity played by both tween boys and girls. Baseball, soccer, and football are next on the boys' list. Soccer and softball follow on the girls' list.

As with sports, tween participation in other activities has also come down since the beginning of the decade. Although holding steady over the past five years, virtually all activities with the exception of a few of the more extreme ones such as skateboarding and in-line skating have suffered drops in tween participation since 1993. Favorite activities for both boys and girls continue to be biking, swimming/diving, rollerblading, and bowling (see Figure 5.4).

One of the steepest declines between 1993 and 2000 occurs in fishing, where a 19 percent decline in tween activity was reported. Given that brand loyalty and habits form during the tween years, you might wonder what will be in store for the fishing equipment market when these

FIGURE 5.2

Average Daily Minutes Tweens Spend Relaxing

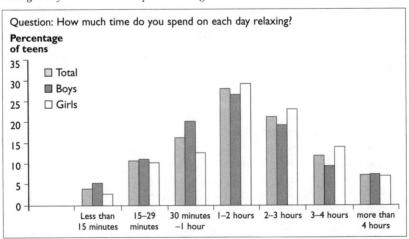

FIGURE 5.3

Sports Played in the Last 12 Months during 2002

SPORT	BOYS	GIRLS
Basketball	57%	35%
Soccer	36	25
Baseball	48	15
Football	36	7
Softball	10	20
Volleyball	12	17
Tennis	10	10

Source: Roper Youth Report 2003

tweens grow into adults. Who will teach their children to fish?

Lastly, tween interest in extreme sports has become sizable among boys with 72 percent of them reporting at least some interest in this venue. In fact, 47 percent of tween boys report being *very* interested in extreme sports (defined as any sport where the participants are doing the activity at dangerous or extreme levels) compared with only 19 percent of tween girls, according to a *Sports Illustrated for Kids* Omnibus Study.

GROUP AFFILIATION

As mentioned earlier, a key motivator in the lives of today's tweens is their desire to belong. They want to fit in with friends as they slowly move away from the childhood and family dependence of an emerging tween, towards the peer dependence more common among transitioning tweens. Again, however, we must remember that they are moving toward this older, group-oriented stage. These kids are far from being totally out of the nest. They may want to get there soon, but they are still very much kids at heart.

FIGURE 5.4

Activities Participated in during the Past Year

Percent of tweens wo reported taking part in these activities in the past year, ranked by 2000		
	1993	2000
Biking	60%	46%
Swimming/diving	56	43
Rollerblading	30	33
Bowling	38	30
Roller Skating	45	28
Running/Jogging	39	26
Skateboarding	17	22
Fishing	36	19
Ice Skating	20	18
Hiking	21	15
Cheerleading	NA	15
Street/Field Hockey	18	13
Horseback Riding	16	11
Karate	NA	10
Snowboarding	NA	9

Source: Feb–May 1993 vs. Feb–May 2000
Sports Illustrated for Kids Omnibus Study

There is a notable difference in how tweens relate to their group compared with how teenagers relate to theirs. Two ads for Union Bay offer a great example of the differences between teenage and tween group affiliation and attitude. The first appeared in teen-oriented *Twist*. The second appeared in *Girls' Life*, whose primary audience is the 8 to 12 year olds. Notice the more serious side in the first teen-oriented ad contrasted by the more fun, still kid-like feel for the second ad oriented to tweens (see Figure 5.5).

FIGURE 5.5
Union Bay Ads

TWEEN PARTICIPATION IN SELECTED ORGANIZATIONS	
Church groups	27%
Little League baseball	13
Other organized sport	11
Scouts (Boy or Girl)	5

Source: Roper Youth Report 2003

Despite their love of fun, fitting in and being part of a group are perhaps more important for today's tweens than for those of a decade ago. Belonging to a group is so important to today's teens and tweens that many ads and TV shows rarely feature lone individuals, according to a study from Next Generation Radio. As part of this desire to affiliate and belong, kids keep at least somewhat busy with groups and clubs. Various reports indicate that at least some of today's tweens continue to grow in spiritual enlightenment.

COMMUNICATION

Today's tween communicates with others far more often and more easily than ever before.

A big part of group affiliation and fitting in is communication, and tweens love to communicate. Today's tween communicates with others far more often and more easily than ever before.

After school, tween girls and boys are likely to hit the Internet and "talk" (Chat, IMing) with their friends. They want to know who is online and want their friends to know that they are online. Our research found that the average online tween girl has a buddy list of about 17 names with 13 percent of transitioning tween girls reporting more than 50 names.

A recent study by SpectraCom and Circle 1 Network found that 32 percent of tweens already have their own cell phones and 56 percent would like to own their own cell phone. They want to make sure that they know where their friends are and what's going on. Moreover, in today's world, this is becoming more difficult to do without the aid of cellular phones. In one particular focus group, one tween girl lamented that she told her friend to reach her at her dad's home. Her friend never called her because she did not know which dad she would be staying with—her biological dad or her stepdad.

Many companies have realized the huge opportunity for satisfying tweens' need for communication. Companies like Tiger, V-Tech, and Girl-Tech are trying to lure this lucrative market with communication devices that send messages within a few hundred feet.

The tween market for personal communication is far from saturated. There is little doubt that as cell phones and pagers become less expensive, more and more tweens will be able to purchase them or successfully influence their parents to buy them.

IMPLICATIONS

- Tweens' busier schedules may warrant the introduction of additional planning and organizing tools to help them schedule days and activities.
- When offering promotional incentives to tweens, cater to their favorite interests: music and nature. Sports could be a strong incentive as well, especially for tween boys.
- Tween chores around the house may suggest new marketing and product opportunities such as special cleaning items or tools for bedroom cleaning and cool, new pet-care products.
- While tweens are constantly on the lookout to affiliate and fit in with peer groups, they are still very much kids at heart. Remember to offer tweens, especially young ones, the benefit of fun.
- Not only are kids future consumers, as Dr. James McNeal advises, they are future teachers and parents as well. Therefore, certain drops in tween activities, such as fishing, could hurt the long-term trend of certain industries. When these tweens become parents, they may not fish as a sport or encourage their children to fish either.

C *h a p t e r*

6

HAPPINESS IS BEING A TWEEN

The vast majority of tweens are very happy today. Surveys of today's tweens reveal that 95 percent feel happy and safe. Interestingly, this is no different than the numbers we found prior to September 11, in our KidzEyes 2000 survey. Furthermore, while fitting in with and being accepted by peers is a primary driver as tweens age upwards, these kids do not outwardly voice discomfort with this task. Of the tweens we interviewed online, 86 percent disagreed with the statement that "friends make me do things I wouldn't normally do."

While they are beginning to express feelings that they may have too much to do everyday, the majority still feel that they have enough free time. While many report having to spend at least some time at home alone during the week, the vast majority (94 percent) feel that they are not left alone at home too much (see Figure 6.1).

In general, today's tweens feel strongly that they are cared for. Virtually all our panel (98 percent) feel that their parents care about them. Most agree that their teachers and friends care about them as well.

In general, today's tweens feel strongly that they are cared for.

Tweens fully expect to have better lives than their parents. Eight in ten tweens agree with the statement "My life will be even better than my parents'." As expected, this will probably occur as a result of having less work pressure because 80 percent feel that their parents now work too hard. In fact, tweens tell us that they are happy with the amount of time they get to spend with their

FIGURE 6.1
Tweens Feel Cared For

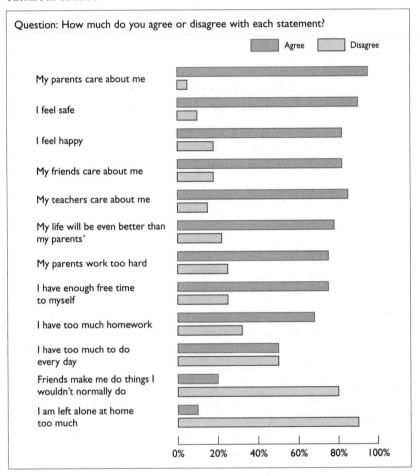

Question: How much do you agree or disagree with each statement?

Agree   Disagree

My parents care about me

I feel safe

I feel happy

My friends care about me

My teachers care about me

My life will be even better than my parents'

My parents work too hard

I have enough free time to myself

I have too much homework

I have too much to do every day

Friends make me do things I wouldn't normally do

I am left alone at home too much

0%   20%   40%   60%   80%   100%

Source: WonderGroup/KidzEyes 2000 Study

working parents, but they wish their parents would be less stressed and tired when they do get to see them. (These are stats from the KidzEyes/ WonderGroup study.)

As for role models, we have constantly seen tweens indicate that their parents, along with entertainers, set the stage. Today's entertainers and sports figures, such as Britney Spears (for girls) and Tiger Woods and Eminem (for boys), are likely to be viewed as leading role models for today's 8 to 12 year olds.

WORRIES AND CONCERNS

The tween world is not all rosy, however, as many tweens voice concerns over various issues that directly, as well as indirectly, affect their lives. For example, the number one concern among tweens is, not surprisingly, "parents dying." Also, while nonexistent in our survey of a few years ago, there is little surprise that "terrorism" has now become the number two tween worry. In addition, tweens are certainly aware of environmental issues and concerned about them: 63 percent of today's tweens report being at least somewhat worried about pollution, and 65 percent are concerned about the environment.

For tween girls, appearance also begins to become a major area of concern. While the majority of kids in this age are generally happy with the way they look, older tweens definitely begin feeling stress over not having the "right" bodies. Bombarded by media, girls in this age range consider the media images of women and older teens as models for themselves. Stress occurs when they realize that their bodies are unable to meet their expectations of what they think society wants them to be.

TWEEN WORRIES AND CONCERNS

Percent Reporting They Are	Worried	At Least Somewhat Worried
Parents dying	39%	81%
Guns in school	23	55
Drugs	21	54
Dying	26	67
Kidnapping	25	66
War	26	77
Fighting in school	11	51
Neighborhood crime	15	55
Pollution	15	63
Environment	16	65
AIDS	14	36
Divorce of parents	16	36
Alcohol	15	39
Being poor	19	55
Being left alone	13	41
Homelessness	15	43
Peer pressure	13	51
Terrorism	29	75
Being sick	11	56
Being overwieight	17	51

Source: WonderGroup/KidzEyes Study 2003

In a study conducted by the Girl Scouts of America, 75 percent of third-grade girls agreed with the statement "I like the way I look," but only 56 percent of seventh-grade girls felt the same.

As concern over appearance rises, so does concern over weight. Girls as young as age 8 speak freely about dieting and watching calories. Our recently-completed 2003 study found more than one out of every two (52 percent) transitioning tween girls agreeing that they should lose weight and more than two out of every three (68 percent) agreeing that they should exercise more. This helps explain why food marketers begin to see significant drops in the consumption of certain sugar-loaded and high-fat products, like sweetened soft drinks and cheese, among girls aged 10 and up.

While both boys and girls experience bodily changes, it is the tween girl that finds this to be most stressful. During the tween years, physical development for girls, such as menstruating and breast enlargement, provide added pressure to become more like teenagers and to give up girlhood before they are ready to do so. Unfortunately, according to today's educators, these tweens are getting little help or understanding from their mothers on how to handle these changes.

When asked to express their greatest fear, a *Sports Illustrated for Kids* study found that tweens' greatest fears centered on death, violence, and animals. (Because this group is in transition from childhood to teenagerhood, this same report also found some more kid-like fears such as monsters, ghosts, and being alone.)

As for the biggest event they've witnessed in the past few years, as expected, tweens were far from oblivious to 9/11 or the war in Iraq. Interestingly, when we surveyed tweens in 1999, they listed "family vacation" as being the biggest event.

GREATEST FEAR (9 TO 11 YEAR OLDS)	Percent reporting
Death of parents, self, family member	14%
Violence (like kidnapping, someone trying to kill them)	14
Accidents (airplane or car crash or heights)	11
Animals (snakes, dogs, spiders)	12
Horror (like monsters, ghosts, and scary movies)	6
The dark/being alone	4

Source: *Sports Illustrated for Kids* Omnibus Study, 1999

BIGGEST EVENTS OF THE PAST FEW YEARS	Percent reporting
The 9/11 terrorist attacks	52%
A family trip or vacation	25
The war in Iraq	13
A sports event	3

Source: WonderGroup/KidzEyes Study 2003

PERCENT OF TWEENS AGREEING "A LOT"		
	8 to 9 year olds	10 to 12 year olds
My teachers care about me.	70%	42%
My friends care about me.	65	50
I feel safe.	75	63
I have enough free time.	42	27

Source: WonderGroup/KidzEyes Study 2003

YOUNG EMERGING AND OLDER TRANSITIONING TWEENS COMPARED

As tweens continue to grow away from childhood and towards being more adult, it is not surprising to see that some attitudes also begin to change. As tweens age, they begin to exhibit more skepticism and a little less happiness in general. As tweens grow older, they tend to believe that teachers may not be caring "that much" about them, or that they are perhaps not getting enough free time, and may not feel as safe or that their friends care about them as much.

MARKETING IMPLICATIONS

- Marketers should remember that younger tweens still hold their teachers in very high regard and therefore might consider marketing efforts aimed towards teachers as well.
- There may be an excellent opportunity for marketers to offer tween girls sound health advice on what to expect and how to better cope with changing physical development.
- Tweens are obviously highly aware of what is happening to society (e.g., drugs, AIDS, guns in schools), so perhaps we will be seeing a move to increased conservatism and control as this group becomes tomorrow's adults.
- This group sees themselves as happy, smart, and successful, and marketers should portray them as so.
- Family togetherness is extremely important. Both tweens and parents may embrace products and promotions that feature this concept.

7

TWEEN EDUCATION ISN'T WHAT IT USED TO BE

We were recently invited to a White House meeting of youth experts sponsored by the Department of Education. The Department of Education is seeking a better understanding of today's kids—Who they are; what they like; what they expect; what they desire; how they interact with technology, peers, and society—as the department develops plans and policies for today's and tomorrow's education system. The charge, as noted by Eugene Hickok, Acting Deputy Secretary, and John Baily, Director, Office of Educational Technology, is "Lets challenge everyone involved to creatively enhance the opportunity for today's kids to learn, and let's keep in mind that schooling should not be confused with education." The nexus of this is that today tweens learn through a number of mediums: classroom teaching, Internet, TV and other video broadcast channels, experiential, extracurricular activities, and many others.

Because much of how tweens learn to think, act, and grow is a result of what they experience in school, it is only right that we take a close look at tween education. How has education changed for tweens over the past few years? How do they spend this important part of their day?

During the past ten years, significant changes have taken place in tween education. Massive changes in society as much as movements in education have fueled these changes and reforms.

Change has come in response to three kinds of influences: first, social equity movements and demographics; second, influences from outside of the United States; and third, the impact of technology and research.

SOCIAL EQUITY MOVEMENTS AND DEMOGRAPHICS

In general, during the past ten years, tweens have been exposed to a more heterogeneous society in school. Elementary school textbooks now include more references to people of color. Librarians have books written by authors with varied ethnic backgrounds. There are now references to more variations of music, and the social studies and history curriculums include broader views of the world. More subtle changes include the appearance of different ethnic groups in casual illustrations and the study of cultural holidays such as Kwanza.

Gender equity has become the norm, both physically and academically. Physical education programs for girls now get an equal share of funding and mirror those for boys, including after-school sports programs. Academic research revealed the existence of subconscious teaching patterns that favored boys over girls. These patterns included calling more often on boys in class and taking for granted that girls were "naturally" not successful or interested in such areas as math and science. The teaching profession now is working to eliminate these biases.

Large, non-English speaking populations, principally Hispanic but also Asian, Central-European, and Middle-Eastern, have a growing influence in the schools. Bilingual programs have emerged to help teach children whose first language is not English. Foreign-language programs and discussions of tolerance have also increased. Children are now able to see their various heritages reflected and are no longer restricted to the image of the dominant, white majority.

In response to the new demands placed on schools, teacher preparation has begun to reflect and reinforce the changes. One of the important changes in teacher preparation is the increased specialization required. School districts, teacher training programs, and state governments now often require teachers to have more depth of knowledge over a shorter range of ages or grades.

A decade or two ago, it was common for teachers to get a certificate that allowed them to teach all subjects in kindergarten through eighth grade, or grades 8 through 12. Now it is more common to have separate certifications for early and late elementary, for middle school (usually grades 5 or 6 through 8), and for high school. While teachers in most elementary school classrooms are still generalists, many states now demand that teachers in middle schools become subject specialists. Some educators argue for increased subject specialization in elementary schools as well.

Over the past decade, schools have begun to address more than just the academic needs of children. Following work by people like James Comer and Edward Ziegler at Yale University, the idea that schools should become comprehensive service centers for all the needs of children began to spread. Some schools now include counseling services, medical clinics, and adult education programs. Drug education programs have become more common, extending down to the elementary school levels where the DARE program ("Say No to Drugs") is now most commonly presented to fifth-grade tweens.

Another influence has been the advent of AIDS and other deadly communicable diseases, such as new strains of the hepatitis virus. In response, schools have developed programs both outside and within classrooms, many of them aimed at tweens. These include sex-education programs as well as an increased emphasis on learning health skills for life such as the importance of exercise, the dangers of alcohol, the effects of smoking tobacco, and the importance of diet.

INFLUENCES FROM OUTSIDE OF THE UNITED STATES

Both educational and noneducational influences from outside the United States continue to affect education in this country.

The first wave of outside influence swept over our educational system in the early 1960s, when the first Russian satellite beeped its way around the world, taking the American space program and public by surprise. This generated a flood of concern that our science, math, engineering, and defense systems were not "keeping up with the Russians," and the education system was the culprit. A generation of new programs aimed mostly at physics, math, and science classes in the high schools was the result.

A more recent influence generating the same kind of anxiety and reactions as the first has been the growth of commercial competition from both developing nations and developed nations looking for markets. The United States is the best market for almost anything. Products ranging from cars and clothing and all kinds of electronic devices are produced abroad and often undersell products made in the United

States. Though vastly oversimplified, this reality has led to further pressure on the U.S. educational system to teach children in ways that prepare them better for the workplace—increasing attention to science and math skills, for example.

Over the past ten years, amidst a plethora of reports that indicated that American students were far behind other countries in a variety of learned skills, the entire field of teaching and learning has been refocused upon student achievement. Meeting a set of content and performance standards at particular points along the formal educational continuum now defines student achievement. Using state-generated or national standards, educators today articulate very clear expectations for every subject and for every child.

THE IMPACT OF TECHNOLOGY AND RESEARCH

In addition to other influences, education is in a state of flux. Direct research on how children learn raises important issues including how to train teachers, the aims and purposes of education, and the tools available to do the job.

Ever since the report called "A Nation at Risk" was published in 1983, educators and others have been taking seriously the task of reinventing the educational system. The work has borne fruit, principally during the past ten years. Although the original report focused more on education in high schools, the outcome produced at least as much impact on the education of students in grades 2 through 6 as it did at other grade levels. Those influences include changes in teacher training and advances in technology, such as the use of computers, the Internet, video, and a shift of resources in schools to "media centers" rather than libraries.

Research and innovation affected the *structure* of education as well. There have been changes in the way students are grouped and in the grade levels served together by different schools. Partly in response to practices in other countries, such as Japan, where school days and years are longer, some districts are increasing the amount of time children spend in school. Schools are experimenting with block scheduling, the practice of having fewer but longer learning periods during the school day. The theory is that even elementary school students learn better in longer blocks of time in which there is more variety in methodology.

Early work by Jean Piaget (see Chapter 1), as well as more recent work on the brain and its functions, has resulted in an increase in thematic teaching. The result is that many more children are learning in a way that focuses them not only on individual skills, but also around a topic, such as Mayan Indians. Around that topic, teachers structure social studies, geography, reading, mathematics, and science.

In addition to changes within schools, many different kinds of schools are being tried. Charter schools, a development of the last ten years, are small, public schools run independently of local school districts. Some center on a basic curriculum. Others follow a "great books" curriculum. Still others center on thematic teaching—sports, technology, or character education, for example. Magnet schools, another public school innovation, are schools that emphasize certain disciplines such as math and science, or music and art.

These newer schools pull students from across district lines. They may help to integrate schools racially without forced busing because attendance at them is purely voluntary. A new breed of schools run for profit by private corporations, and a movement to give vouchers to parents so they can use their education taxes to send their children to private schools round out the picture.

Along with improved teaching research has come the introduction of technology into the classroom. Improved technology and use of the Internet in today's schools give today's tweens access to more information and creativity than their predecessors had. These improvements alone may lead to the best-educated generation of kids ever and, thereby, to the savviest consumers ever. New learning system software can customize instruction to specific students' needs and offer pinpoint prescriptives. Algorithms can now be written to guide students to specific remedial instruction when making a mistake such as incorrectly adding two numbers.

At the same time, technology is beginning to offer parents of today's tweens a way to better monitor their children and their schools' progress. Schools are offering their own Web sites that mom and dad can use to check for their children's homework assignments and even check their children's grades. Computers can track all student data, helping teachers and parents better understand each student's strengths and weaknesses.

Special Internet services are now being provided to tween and teen classrooms. These help students navigate and use the Web in ways that are especially relevant to their education, providing them with a powerful search engine that brings together sites that are educationally relevant as well as online encyclopedias and other resources. Services like these are provided either for a fee or, in some instances, in return for school acceptance of paid advertising that appears on the Internet site.

Technology not only includes computers and the Internet but also changes in medicine and treatment that have had an impact on elementary schools. For example, there is increased use of chemical controls such as Ritalin and other drugs to manage hyperactivity and attention deficit disorder (ADD). Along with that come more children in classrooms who are medicated for various other behavioral and learning disorders. And as asthma is an increasingly common condition among kids, a large and growing number of elementary school children are using inhalers in school.

The picture of what is happening in the education of our students in grades 2 through 6 is clearly complex and changing. The effects of technology, the impact of disease, medication and drugs, and of new educational theories have never been more complex.

TODAY'S TWEEN CURRICULUM

Curricula for tween-aged grades (2 through 6) reflect the following four major goals of education:

1. Academic
2. Vocational Career, Including Technology
3. Social, Civic, and Economic
4. Personal Development

During these formative years, students are engaged in activities that provide the rudiments of educational skills, while being encouraged to develop the foundations for deeper levels of thinking and problem solving for their progress into the upper grades.

Academic

Today's tweens are taught not only how to read and write, but also to do basic research and analysis, and to respond to various types of written and oral materials in appropriate ways. Students are encouraged to use what they already know, identify what they want to know, and then explore what they want to learn. This encourages them to identify and select appropriate materials and create meaningful connections among them.

Today's tweens use their creativity to write and design brochures, presentations, narratives, videos, storyboards, mind-maps, and animated presentations. They are likely to perform dramas and use instrumental, environmental, or electronically generated sound effects. They may create Web sites or contribute their work to existing Web sites. These new avenues pique the interests of students at the same time they exercise unique approaches to learning and prepare students to function as workers within the broad society.

Today's tweens use their creativity to write and design brochures, presentations, narratives, videos, storyboards, mind-maps, and animated presentations.

It is also during tween education that children begin mastering numbers or "numeracy." *Numeracy* calls upon students to recognize, understand, and be able to do simple manipulations of objects and numerical concepts. Students learn the basic operations such as addition, subtraction, multiplication, and division. They learn how to survey their classmates and graph the responses. Some upper-elementary (fifth-grade and sixth-grade) students, who are ready, are introduced to basic algebraic formulas and the world of conceptual mathematical manipulation.

In the elementary grades, teachers highlight the fine and graphic arts, linear and creative thinking skills, interpersonal skills, and reflection and self-correction skills. The goal here is to reach children through stimulating exercises that use their creative and intellectual prowess. Providing students with real-world problems related to their environment or communities exposes them to learning that is not only cognitively important, but useful and meaningful as well.

Vocational/Career, Including Technology

Increasingly, we see elementary classroom teachers use children's interest in vocations (although still high-profile ones like police officer, sports star, and lawyer) to stimulate student interest in subject matter. For example, a link may be made between a popular race car driver, his or her car design, and scientific concepts dealing with wind resistance. Students are often asked to work through word problems, measure, calculate, graph, and learn other useful skills that can transfer to the workplace.

The recognition that many American jobs require teamwork, not individual work, has lead to an increased emphasis on learning in teams.

The recognition that many American jobs require teamwork, not individual work, has lead to an increased emphasis on learning in teams. More often, teachers are bringing together students of diverse strengths to work on projects, particularly because children with special needs are now included in regular classrooms. This is helping students to become more open-minded, less afraid of those who are different from them, and more focused on accomplishing goals through interdependence as well as individual ingenuity. In working through problems and learning to collaborate with their peers, today's students are developing better real-world vocational skills than students have developed in past generations.

It has also become an important role of today's schools to ensure that kids become familiar and comfortable with technology and the Internet. According to Ms. Lee Scharback, certified special education and speech/language pathologist and formerly the head of education for the Connecting with Kids Network, "The big issue today is how do educators embrace the technology and use it in education?" In 1999, national educational technology standards were developed for Internet literacy and technology skills. Information regarding these standards as well as other technology policies are detailed in the Department of Education's National Education Technology Plan (http://www.NationalEdTechPlan.org).

The educational goals in the area of information technology are all directed toward helping students become independent, competent, and confident users. Students must be able to acquire basic skills and content, communicate ideas, solve problems, and pursue personal interests. At the elementary level, students begin to learn about the technology through fun activities that teach them keyboard skills. Later, they learn to locate information and learn specific applications such as word processing.

As tweens move from the second grade through the sixth grade, they use information and technology for problem solving and communication. They choose and organize materials with greater efficiency and determine the effectiveness and efficiency of their choices and decisions. They learn to apply the technologies to create written, visual, oral, and multimedia presentations to communicate their ideas, information, or conclusions to others.

A very important outcome of tweens and computers, Internet access particularly, is that today's tweens are taught to investigate the validity of information they gather. After all, not everything on the Internet is true. This skeptical approach to information is certainly affecting their perception of advertising.

Technology is the one area where teachers continually struggle to stay ahead of some of their students.

Technology is the one area where teachers continually struggle to stay ahead of some of their students. According to Lee Scharback, "When it comes to much of technology, kids know more than teachers." In addition, today's kids expect technology applications in schools to be as current as the console games, such as Nintendo and other electronic games and programs they have at home. There is no question that more wireless curriculum is on the way. According to Ms. Scharback, "Tweens now expect that they can keep assignments on Palm Pilots versus homework pads. Soon students will expect to have entire books on their Palm Pilots."

Social, Civic, and Economic

Throughout elementary school, students are taught to think and solve problems, gather historical, geographical, and civic data, engage in primary source reading and information gathering techniques such as interviews and surveys, and make sense of timelines and the human continuum.

Students in the lower grades are introduced to the U.S. Constitution and the basics of how the U.S. system of government works. They learn about the values of liberty and living in a multicultural society where diversity is valued. Activities include making three-dimensional maps, planning bake sales (to simulate supply and demand), operating school stores, mentoring younger children, generating plays about historical figures, and celebrating diverse heritages through the arts or the stories of grandparents and other significant adults in the lives of the children.

As students near the sixth grade, they begin to practice writing persuasive compositions, stating their opinions and identifying supportive evidence. These skills help them work through complex questions and understand the processes necessary for justice to occur. In this way, they learn to become fully functional members of a broader society.

To further student understanding of their role in the future, a greater emphasis on geography, world languages, and peoples is rapidly becoming a focal point in elementary classrooms. Students in the lower elementary grades learn about cultural traditions that transmit beliefs and ideals, as well as family support and economic life within different countries around the world. They begin to explore the reasons behind migration of large groups of people. By learning about trade among nations children are introduced to economics.

To further student understanding of their role in the future, a greater emphasis on geography, world languages, and peoples is rapidly becoming a focal point in elementary classrooms.

Personal Development

With today's kids' exposure to so much media, free time, and less parental supervision, schools have had to take on a more aggressive role as advisor and protector in the area of personal development.

Schools systems tend to focus on the following four areas of personal development:

1. Living a healthy and active life
2. Dealing with injury and disease
3. Human growth and development
4. Substance abuse and prevention

In each of these areas, students in the elementary years learn to identify resources, access them adequately, and use them effectively.

In learning to live a healthy and active life, all students are required to have physical education classes as part of their routine school experience. This helps encourage them to have daily physical activity, learn interpersonal skills, and learn about stress reduction and management.

As students progress through elementary school, they also learn about nutrition. They are asked to plan and select nutritious meals, based on the U.S. dietary guidelines, and develop a plan to maintain their own healthy weight as they continue to grow, noting what foods help develop strong muscles and bones. Students learn to identify several types of health problems associated with poor food choices and eating habits. They learn to look at ways in which they can manage the influences on our lifestyles from the media and pop culture.

Children learn safety, both physical and emotional, at home and at school. Lessons center on recognizing unsafe conditions, avoiding risk-taking activities that cause intentional or unintentional injury or disease, and handling emergencies. Schools teach basic first aid techniques throughout elementary school. Among the topics are basic CPR techniques, how to help a choking victim, and how to prevent poisoning. Students also must demonstrate the skills necessary for avoiding dangerous situations. In addition, they learn basic science about the safe use of electricity and fire.

Students are taught about the importance of obtaining information and help from parents, health professionals, clergy, and other responsible adults. They are asked to demonstrate the skills necessary to resolve conflicts peacefully. Last but not least, students learn to recognize the power of their own abilities to make good choices to reduce or eliminate health risks.

Educators often focus on the influence of media in shaping popular culture. They want students to recognize the influence of these images and messages on their personal choices. This is especially important in the area of substance abuse and prevention. Students learn about the dangers of using alcohol, tobacco, and other drugs, and they identify strategies for avoiding these in their own lives. Children in early elementary school learn about drugs with simple and positive messages and progress to more in-depth work as they move into the upper-elementary and middle-school years.

As early as kindergarten, students learn the basics of interacting with other children in a classroom and begin the process of self-discipline. By the second grade, students are expected to maintain a modicum of self-control and self-restraint so that they can learn and allow others to learn within the classroom setting. Children learn ways of demonstrating and communicating care, concern, and consideration.

In the upper-elementary grades, students learn about some of the emotional and physical changes that will occur during puberty. Throughout the grade levels, students are taught about different and appropriate ways to express emotions, so that a healthy manner is established. The disciplines of using exercise to release energy, writing reflectively, giving and receiving feedback, and concentrating are all taught overtly in many of today's classrooms.

SHORTFALLS

While schools must now do more in the areas of teaching and guiding development than ever before, there are still reports of shortfalls resulting largely from inadequate funding. There are gaps between what technology can offer and what schools possess. There is, as some educators say, a digital divide. Some schools have money and others do not. Fran Kick, educational consultant and author, states, "By 2005, well over 90 percent of schools in this country will have T1 access. Now, it'll be varied in terms of who gets to see that T1 access, but at least the pipe will be in the schoolhouse door." He adds, "The technology's there. But, some of that hardware is being put in schools that have leaky roofs and asbestos and terrible ventilation systems."

One of our advisors, a third-grade teacher in a poor Hispanic area of San Francisco, confirmed the problem. She explained that although some of the classrooms in her school finally have Internet access, their computers are too old to take advantage of it. When we provided a table full of arts and crafts materials for a new-product-idea session, she exclaimed, "There are more supplies on this table for one day than the supply I get for the entire school year!"

In general, schools need assistance including free and up-to-date curriculum materials. According to the National Education Association, typical school districts spend only 1 percent of their budgets on books and materials. In fact, we often hear of elementary school teachers who reach into their own (sometimes poorly paid) pockets in order to buy supplies for their classrooms. In 2001, teachers reportedly spent an average of $521 of their own money (up from $480 in 1998) to buy books, art supplies, materials for experiments, and more.

IN-SCHOOL MARKETING

These shortfalls have created win-win situations for some marketers and educational institutions. Many schools need funds, supplies, and teaching aids. Likewise, many businesses need to reach students inside of classrooms. Consequently, many schools and teachers are now open to accepting help in the form of money, supplies, and teaching aids in return for allowing in-school marketing efforts that they deem acceptable and appropriately unassertive.

Because many elementary school teachers are looking for help in supplying their classrooms and finding better teaching aids, teachers represent an important channel for reaching today's tweens. According to Don Lay, president of LearningWorks, an educational marketing firm, there are more than 1 million elementary school teachers, 800,000 of whom teach the tween grades of 2 through 6. Many of these teachers are reachable through e-mail and other direct marketing efforts.

In some areas, school districts have been able to raise significant, much-needed funds from beverage bottlers who provide money in return for having their vending machines in the schools (with a recent shift from carbonated drinks to juice beverage offerings). In other situations, schools have elected to receive free printing of lunch menus in return for advertising support.

Many companies offer teachers lesson plans and other in-class activities in return for small sponsorship or logo designations appearing somewhere within the program. Response to these programs has been favorable for both teachers and companies alike.

ESTIMATED NUMBER OF ELEMENTARY SCHOOL TEACHERS IN THE UNITED STATES

Grade	Number of Teachers
First	200,000
Second	190,000
Third	180,000
Fourth	165,000
Fifth	156,000
Sixth	122,000
Total	**1,013,000**
Number of Elementary Schools	**64,500**

Source: LearningWorks 2000

An example of such a program is the Chiquita in-school program. To raise student awareness of Chiquita bananas, Chiquita Brands worked with WonderGroup and LearningWorks to find a way to assist teachers and, at the same time, fit Chiquita bananas in with the elementary-school curriculum. The company found that teachers would welcome assistance and materials associated with teaching about Central America—the key area where bananas are grown. Chiquita provided teachers with the following:

- A four-page, two-color teacher's guide
- Four dual-sided, reproducible student activities (oriented by grades 1 to 3 and 4 to 6)
- Chiquita song sheets
- Banana stickers (for rewards)
- A full-color wall poster
- A teacher-response card

Follow-up research indicated a strong win-win situation for both Chiquita and the participating schools. More than 28,000 programs were distributed, and, on average, four teachers in each school used each program and shared it with more than 100 students. As a result, an estimated 2.8 million students became involved with the brand. Teachers were pleased with the assistance, providing comments like the following:

- "Everything is great and it's free—thank you Chiquita."
- "Great asset to my unit on the Rain Forest."
- "Program is motivation for me and fun for my students."
- "Poster is terrific—it's the only one I've seen on Central America."

For Chiquita, the student interaction with and exposure to the brand was exceptional. Almost all teachers used Chiquita stickers as rewards, associating Chiquita bananas as a reward or signal of excellence. Almost all of the teachers used at least one activity and gave out "Chiquita" certificates of accomplishment. In addition, every classroom displayed the wall poster—which included a small but very visible "Miss Chiquita" (see Figure 7.1).

TIPS FOR MARKETERS

In developing in-school programs, it is important to keep in mind the following basics:

FIGURE 7.1

Destination Central America Poster

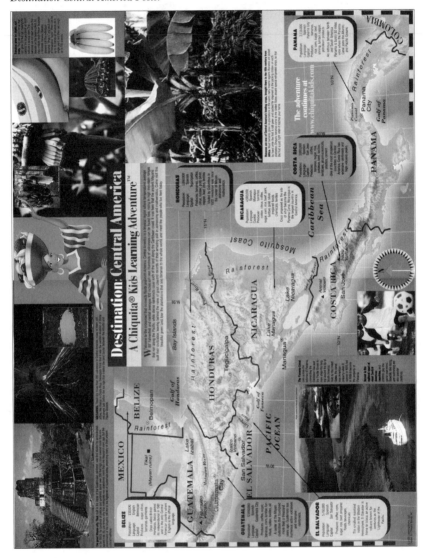

- Know the curriculum at different grade levels and develop programs that are grade and subject appropriate.
- Understand the seasonality of the school year. Find out when various themes and subjects are taught. Programs should be targeted to these dates.

- Make materials easy to use for teachers and administrators. They are very busy people.
- Make sure that you are truly offering something educational and be careful not to step over the line of being too commercial.
- Think like a parent! As a parent, would you be thankful to the sponsor for providing this assistance to your school and to your children? Would you want class time taken to implement it?

IMPLICATIONS

- Tweens are being taught to expect a world that is culturally diverse. Advertising would be wise to reflect this.
- Tweens are becoming technologically adept at younger ages—a trend that will continue.
- Today's tweens expect to be able to easily access whatever information they desire concerning various products and services they wish to buy or investigate. Marketers should make certain that appropriate Web sites are developed and made accessible to these potential consumers.
- To keep up with the newest standards and advances in Internet literacy, marketers should monitor http://www.iste.org, the Web site of the International Society for Technology in Education.
- Tweens are much savvier than their predecessors in understanding advertising and the media. Smart marketers should remember that these tweens expect the facts not just the sizzle.
- In-school marketing can be a worthwhile addition to your marketing mix, providing that you identify the appropriate teacher needs.
- Marketing, advertising, and sponsorship opportunities may exist on various school Web sites that are frequented daily by students and their parents.
- New opportunities for marketing to teachers now exist by advertising on or sponsoring various teacher Web sites.

8

TWEEN FAVORITES
Food, Music, Fashion, and Toys

TWEENS AND FOOD

A frequent question we receive from food marketers is: "Just how involved are today's tweens in choosing or making their own meals? After all, we know that mom is the primary purchaser so shouldn't we address all our marketing messages to her?"

Moms may purchase most of the food for their households, but tweens are a major factor in this market category. Generally, if it goes into a tween's mouth, it has to first get past his or her defenses. In Chapter 4, we studied the impact that positive and negative influences have on a mom's potential to purchase a product for her child. Nowhere does that influence have more impact than in the food category because a mom knows what the tween has eaten (or not eaten) merely by looking in her cabinet.

In today's households, tweens make quite a few of the meals they eat. In fact, the vast majority of tweens are solely responsible for making their own breakfasts. A significant share of tweens make their own lunches, and some even make their own dinners. There is no chance that tweens will make their own meal with food that they themselves do not like. Moreover, today's busy mom is not going to buy food for her tween if she knows her tween will not eat it.

Not only do tweens make their own meals, in some cases, they actually make the family meal. Surprisingly,

Not only do tweens make their own meals, in some cases, they actually make the family meal.

TWEEN MEALS Percent of 8 to 12 year-olds who make their meals at least once a week		
	Boys	**Girls**
Breakfast	74%	79%
Lunch	51	64
Dinner	23	30
Meal for family	17	30

Source: WonderGroup/KidzEyes 2003 Survey

30 percent of tween girls and 17 percent of tween boys report making the family meal at least once a week.

The After-School Snack

Possibly the most important food time for tweens is the after-school snack. Many tween focus groups have told us that after school is their favorite time of day because it is at that time that they almost totally control what they get to eat. And, eat they do!

When they are not in after-school programs, the majority of tweens get home between 3 P.M. and 4 P.M., and 31 percent of tweens report that the very first thing they do when they get home is eat. Focus groups conducted with tweens about this particular time of day reveal that they get home from school "almost famished" and feeling almost totally out of energy.

In fact, 91 percent of tweens surveyed reported making their own after-school snack at least once during the week and almost half (44 percent) reported making their own snack everyday or almost everyday.

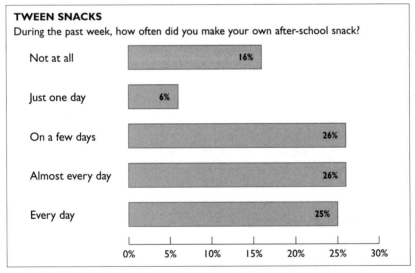

TWEEN SNACKS
During the past week, how often did you make your own after-school snack?

Not at all	16%
Just one day	6%
On a few days	26%
Almost every day	26%
Every day	25%

Source: KidzEyes/WonderGroup Internet panel, December 2000

What's a Snack?

Obviously this tween-snacking occasion is an opportunity for food marketers. But it is important to realize that the competition here is huge.

Just about everything edible is considered a good snacking candidate by today's tweens. In fact, according to our tweens, the best snack is something that tastes good (usually sweet), satisfies hunger (but is not so filling that mom will think that it will ruin supper), and is a quick pick-me-up. In addition, focus group results find that tweens already know that just about all foods will give them energy. Most foods can fill the bill here. Snack chips, cakes, fruits, breakfast foods, leftovers, and anything microwaveable are all considered fine snacking options.

Favorite Foods

Virtually every time we test for tween preferences in flavors, certain ones continually rise to the top. Pizza flavor is the traditional big winner for snacks, sauces, and many food items. Chocolate is a big additive to just about anything. Grape, red (Yes—red is a flavor!), and berry (doesn't matter—just berry) are also popular flavors. Then there is "cheese!" Cheesier . . . nacho . . . quesadilla . . . the more cheese the better!

As for beverages, cola still rules. Surprisingly, bottled water is second to cola, at least for tween girls.

Here's a general caution about high-fat, deliciously sugary products. Watch out. We are seeing a serious drop in the appeal of these items among transitioning tween girls. Body image and concerns begin to take root at this age. Certain high-fat foods, such as cheese, and sugary drinks take a nosedive in popularity among girls of this latter tween age.

Implications

Food marketers should consider greater availability of snack-sized portions to capitalize on tween-snacking occasions.

Food marketers might have opportunities to position their current offerings to tweens as excellent snack alternatives. All food marketers must remember to elicit kid reactions and not just mom reactions to new food products.

If possible, food marketers should advertise to tweens so that they know of the product and its benefit to them.

Packaging for food items should be kid-friendly to allow tweens to use the product more easily by themselves.

Watch out for high-fat, high-sugar products if trying to target older tween girls.

Because tweens make some of their own meals, pay particular attention to making products that are easy to prepare. Tweens may not always have mom's help in the kitchen.

TWEENS AND FASHION

During the tween years, an interesting transition takes place on the cultural front. Kids go from wearing clothes and listening to music selected by their parents, to having a personal, vested interest in their own fashions and music. When you combine this personal interest with their allowances and influence, you can see why fashion manufacturers, retailers, and the music industry are clamoring to cater to tweens. It means many dollars to the retailers who are tapping into the desires of this younger generation.

It is at this age that we especially see girls become very interested in shopping for their clothes. As one 10 year old recently told us, "I first discovered I liked shopping when I actually found a store I liked and clothes that fit and that I liked. I don't remember the exact date, but when I was around 8 I just started enjoying spending money on new things that I could use."

To see just how excited tween girls get about shopping for clothes, we have included two pictures in Figure 8.1 that were among many drawn for us during recently conducted focus groups on the subject of shopping for clothes. As the drawings illustrate, these girls see shopping as tremendous fun. Look at the filled shopping bags, the big smiles, the store names, the shopper saying, "Wow!"

According to many industry surveys, most of the brands tweens say are "coolest" are soft-goods retail brands. Following soft goods are electronics, soft drink, and automotive (yes, automotive) brands. Tweens consistently name soft-goods retail brands ranging from Nike and Adidas to Old Navy and Tommy Hilfiger as the coolest brands.

According to *Women's Wear Daily* (April 2003), industry analysts estimated that for the year 2003 apparel retail sales for tween girls will reach 5.5 billion (teen girls will spend 12.6 billion). If we take this retail apparel spending and divide it by the number of tween girls, approximately 10.5 million, we come up with an average apparel spending level

FIGURE 8.1

Tweens Go Shopping

of $525 per girl. Some of this $525 is directly from the pockets of these tweens, and a larger portion is from their parents' wallets. This spending is only for girls' clothing. Add spending for boys' clothing as well as the other retail categories, and you can see why retailers pay attention to tweens. Also note, the more traditional department store retailers are taking their cues from the specialty retailers. Stores such as Mervyn's, Macy's, and Bloomingdale's are patterning departments after the specialty retailers that have embraced this group, including Limited Too, Abercrombie & Fitch, and Old Navy.

Retailers now offer a broad array of products that are designed, and displayed in-store, specifically with the tween in mind. Soft-goods retailers offer accessories, cosmetics, room décor, and lifestyle products in order to appeal to a tween's sense of style and in order to promote multiple purchases once they are in the store. Julie Fein Azoulay, writing for *Children's Business* (August 1999), brings to life the retail importance of cross-merchandising. She states, "The key to powerful cross-merchandising lies in the concept environment. To be effective, cross-merchandising should create an atmosphere that's fun, funky or powerfully 'now.' That environment could be as small as a register countertop or as big as an entire store . . . but see it as a world that means something to your target tween and you'll understand the key to attracting the tween consumer."

Another thing retailers have learned over the past few years is that, to many tweens, shopping is an environmental experience, and thus the retail environment must meet this need. Limited Too is a good example

of a retailer that has evolved from a place to buy clothes to a place to be immersed in "tweendom." At Limited Too, girls can sample nail polish and make-up, try on clothes, and try out fun blow-up furniture for their rooms. They can use the photo booth to have pictures of themselves made into stickers, look through popular tween magazines, and top the experience off with their favorite candy. Another retailer that has embraced this generation is Target. Target generally allocates more space for its junior department and positions it in more prominent locations within the store than its primary competitors. Target also offers an extensive assortment of merchandise for tweens, including its own brand, Xhilaration, and even private-label cosmetics from make-up artists such as Sonia Kashuk.

Even Saks Fifth Avenue is getting into the act with its recent acquisition of Club Libby Lu, a funky boutique chain that targets tween girls with fashion, customizable make-up, and fun hairstyle makeovers. Current plans call for expanding stand-alone mall storefronts as well as a roll-out of store-within-a-store concepts in existing Saks Fifth Avenue locations.

Where else do tweens like to shop? In a December 2000 study by WonderGroup on fashion apparel shopping, tweens indicated that they shopped for clothes at a number of retailers (Figure 8.2). This table demonstrates that the all-family purchase dynamic still plays a large role in the retail experience of tweens. America's families shop at Wal-Mart. Thus, it makes sense that it is a strong retail destination for tweens.

However, the table also demonstrates the influence of tweens. Almost 40 percent of all girls shop at the Limited Too, a premium-priced specialty retailer that relies on tweens to ask their moms to take them to the store. Even more significant, this store is not even available yet in all locations.

A similar study by *Sports Illustrated for Kids*, completed in December 1999, included boys. The boys named the store that they considered the best place to buy everyday clothes. The results are shown in Figure 8.3.

The stores indicated by boys also follow a pattern of family-based purchase dynamics. Of interest is the high percentage of stores that fall into the classic department store retail category. These

FIGURE 8.2

Where Tweens Like to Shop

Wal-Mart	88%
Kmart	85
Target	81
JCPenney	73
Sears	71
Kids 'R Us	60
Old Navy	58
Gap	49
Limited Too	38
Abercrombie & Fitch	10
Online	10

Source: KidzEyes/WonderGroup Internet Panel, December 2000

FIGURE 8.3

*Boys Choose the Best Place
To Buy Clothes*

Old Navy	11%
JCPenney	9
Gap	8
Kmart	6
Wal-Mart	5
Mervyn's	5
Sears	4
Dillards	4
American Eagle Outfitters	3
Target	2
Macy's	2
Abercrombie & Fitch	2
Pacific Sunwear	2

Source: *Sports Illustrated for Kids*, December 1999

stores have done a good job at featuring and merchandising brands that appeal to tween boys, such as the Tommy brand.

Not included in the list are specialty retailers that cater to a specific category. These include such specialties as accessories (Claire's), cosmetics (Bath & Body Work's Art Stuff brand), home furnishings (Pottery Barn Kids), furniture (E.A. Kids by Ethan Allen), as well as catalog and online retailers.

dELiA*s, a catalog retailer, has become very successful in a short time by focusing on tween and teen girls. We have heard girls say that the day after the dELiA*s catalog arrives, everyone brings their catalog to school to talk about the fashions, accessories, and home furnishings that are featured throughout the book.

In a *Philadelphia Inquirer* article titled "Is room décor the next hot thing for teens and tweens?" Diane Goldsmith describes the room of a Cherry Hill, NJ, girl: "Rachel Fieldman's bedroom is filled with posters of soccer and music stars, such as Mia Hamm and Avril Lavigne, dance imagery, and a blow-up chair with a pillow shaped like the *SpongeBob SquarePants* character, Patrick Star. Rachel found her sheets and pillowcases in the dELiA*s catalog, the ones that read repeatedly, even hypnotically, 'Eyes getting heavy . . . very sleepy'."

In a *Washington Post* article titled "Targeting Tweens: Marketers finding room to grow," Jura Knocius describes the bedroom of a 10-year-old girl named Danielle.

Danielle Brand spends hours listening to music on her new silver CD player in her peach-and-purple Bethesda [Maryland] bedroom. Danielle, 10, loves shiny stuff. Her organdy-covered vanity table, which once belonged to her great-grandmother, is loaded with glitter gels, and sparkling hair mascara. A transparent inflatable chair is filled with sparkly confetti; the walls are painted with gold stars. Several treasured collections are displayed on glass shelves and in wire baskets: Beanie Babies, Venetian puppets and gymnastic medals. "My room is very special to me. My friends come over, and we like to hang out or listen to music" says Danielle. "Sometimes, I think I'm getting too old for this print," she adds, pointing out the flowery duvet cover and dust ruffle she's had since she was 3. That's how it starts. The emerging decorating mantra of the tween: Banish the babyish, bring on the cool.

But how do tweens decide what is cool to wear?

In another study that supports the figures at right, parents acknowledge that their tweens understand brands and are adept at making shopping decisions. In a 1998 study by Penn, Schoen & Berland Associates, it was reported, "Many parents believe their kids know more about brands than [they as parents do] in a variety of product categories." The study also found that 69 percent of parents say that they talk to their child about purchases before going shopping, and that this increases to 88 percent if purchasing a product for the child. This is supported by a newer information from the 2003 Yankelovich Youth MONITOR which states that 68 percent of parents believe "it makes my shopping easier when my child [aged nine to 11] knows what brands he likes."

Many of these savvy tween shoppers are still looking for social cues that indicate what is popular, while also starting to rely on their own opinions. It is clear that tweens are the keeper of purchases regarding what they wear, either as direct purchases or as influencers when they shop with their parents.

In recognition that today's kids have become the predominant decision-makers in determining their own fashion purchases, the print media has proliferated with publications catering to the tween's need to know. *Teen People, Teen, Girls Life, YM, Seventeen, Cosmo Girl, Cheerleader, dELiA*s* (a catalog), and many other publications commit large portions of their magazines to editorial content elated to fashion, fashion design, cosmetics, and personal care. Additionally, youth magazines such as *Disney Adventures, Sports Illustrated for Kids,* and *Nickelodeon* carry ads for Ralph Lauren Kids, Gap Kids, and Nordstrom.

An article by Ruth La Ferla in *The New York Times* notes,

A survey of 1,484 tweens, aged 8 to 12 revealed:	
How do you decide what is cool to wear?	
What I like most	50%
Magazines & TV	22
Other kids my age	21
Older brother or sister	7
Who picks the new clothes you buy?	
I do	47%
Pick out together	40
Mom or dad	13

Source: Children's Broadcasting Corporation

More traditional girls' magazines are racing to exploit the new generation's penchant for living large, a message imbibed everywhere from music videos to style channels on television to affluent parents. *Seventeen* magazine, read by many transitioning tweens, mailed a 32-page supplement with its October 2000 issue called "On the Edge," which highlights vanguard trends and merchandise rarely showcased in the parent publication. Among them: a racy vinyl slicker and matching skirt by D&G and hip-again Burberry plaids.

In the same article, La Ferla quoted Jane Rinzler Buckingham, who heads Youth Intelligence, a trend-spotting firm,

> Kids today are so self-assured. They also tend to make buying decisions on their own. It's no longer a question of "Please, Mom, can I have this?" but "I really want this, and I'll earn the money to get it."

An article in *Women's Wear Daily* titled "Kids take on high-end fashion" states,

> At first we thought it was kind of a fluke when we spotted teens and even tweens sporting the high-end designer labels. But alas, it's most definitely not . . . younger kids have suddenly turned to luxury when it comes to buying clothes and accessories. . . . With this new fashion mind set, kids' tastes are changing. They know a chintzy material when they feel it and can tell if that necklace isn't sterling silver. Manufacturers who design specifically for this age group are hustling to introduce the more expensive fabrics and leathers, hoping to keep up with these fancy new tastes.

Quality and branding are continuing to grow as determining factors in their perception of what is cool, and what products they are going to buy.

We don't think that this trend for high-end fashions means that tweens are going to stop shopping at Wal-Mart and shift en masse to Nieman Marcus. However, it does signify that tweens are becoming more fashion conscious, and that quality and branding are continuing to grow as determining factors in their perception of what is cool, and what products they are going to buy.

TWEENS AND THEIR MUSIC

Singing songs with parents, at preschool programs, and along with television programs such as *Barney, Sesame Street,* and *KidsSongs,* brought positive music experiences to today's tweens. Upon reaching the emerging tween years, these older kids begin to appreciate that there are various types of music and that it is okay to like some forms of music but not others. At this age, the battle for control of the car radio or CD player begins in earnest with their parents—a battle that will continue through their teen years.

In the 2003 KidsEyes Psychographic Study, tweens continue to report pop music as their favorite type of music, but not at the same levels as was reported in the first edition of *The Great Tween Buying Machine.* In a 2000 study by *Sports Illustrated for Kids* we saw 37 percent of those polled state that pop was their favorite music format, in the 2003 study by KidsEyes, only 31 percent favored pop. The second most favorite musical format was rap, followed by country, hip-hop, rock, and Christian rock. Farther down the line were oldies, R&B, alternative rock, and heavy metal.

The same survey asked tweens to name their favorite musicians and groups. Eminem, Avril Lavigne, and Nelly led the pack. This shows the new diversity in music that is in tune with today's youth—rap, rock, and hip-hop. The next three favorites are holdovers from the pop acts that topped the charts three years ago: Backstreet Boys, Britney Spears, and *NSync. The top ten list is rounded out by Jennifer Lopez, Aaron Carter, Shania Twain, and Bow Wow. Aaron Carter, the young pop singer whose older brother is Nick Carter of the Backstreet Boys, and Bow Wow, are among a number of new, young artists that have specifically targeted tweens with growing success. Aaron and Bow Wow have sold millions of records worldwide, and they are both just 16 years old. Bow Wow has already perfected the spin of public relations showmanship and merchandising that connects with this age group. He has already hit the big screen as star of 20th Century Fox's hit *Like Mike,* and he recently announced the launch of his own clothing line. Another young rapper who is following suit is Lil Romeo, again already a musical success. The son of rapper Master P is now appearing in his own show on Nickelodeon titled *Romeo!* Hilary Duff, star of Disney's *Lizzie McGuire,* just released her first album, *Metamorphoses,* to an audience of tweens that adore her and her show.

Girls were almost twice as likely to cite pop as their favorite format as compared to boys, and girls also ranked higher in preference for hip-hop, country, and Christian rock. Boys ranked higher preferences for rap (30 percent compared to 22 percent) and were twice as likely to cite rock as their favorite format compared with girls.

An interesting phenomenon that seems to have encouraged the intensity of music involvement by tweens is the large number of current acts that are themselves tweens and teens. Although some of the acts have members who are now in their twenties, most started in their teens. This contrasts dramatically with the music that is more popular with their parents. These tweens can readily note the current popular bands of their boomer parents—who are listening to the "oldies" from the 1980s—as music for them versus music for us. Some of the most popular music acts today, and the new emerging acts, are young and have strong connections to tweens, including:

- Bow Wow (16 years old)
- Aaron Carter (16 years old)
- Hilary Duff (16 years old)
- Avril Lavigne (18 years old)
- Michelle Branch (19 years old)

Not since the 1960s has there been such a proliferation of very young musicians with commercial success as there has been over the past five years. Something to remember is that groups from the 1960s are still playing music, generating albums, and dearly embraced by the Boomers. These tweens may well bring their musicians along with them into adulthood. Interestingly, many of the names noted in this same listing for the first edition of *The Great Tween Buying Machine* have continued to be popular acts, in fact taking their audiences with them. Britney Spears, Christina Aguilera, Justin Timberlake (*NSync), and Beyonce Knowles (Destiny's Child) have all had recent successful albums now with older audiences.

Adept marketers capitalize in many ways on tweens' interest in music. Opportunities exist to gain attention, validity, and significance by tapping into contemporary music that connects with tweens. Some ways to do this are discussed below.

Music in Communications

The use of contemporary music styles in communications signifies that your product or service is for the youth market. We have noticed a growing number of marketers who are incorporating light rap jingles and pop music backgrounds in their television and radio commercials.

Act or Music Tour Sponsorships

Sponsorships are discussed in more length in Chapter 12, "Finding Tweens at the Grassroots Level." Companies gain brand recognition and awareness by associating with popular tours, such as Johnson & Johnson's Shampoo sponsorship of the 2000 "All That and More" music tour for tweens.

Promotions

Relevant in-and-out marketing opportunities exist to push trial, purchase, or traffic by managing promotional giveaways or events with popular acts. In 2000, Burger King successfully promoted its Burger King Kids program with a strong tie-in with the Backstreet Boys. The music group appeared in BK Kids television commercials promoting a purchase-with-purchase premium of a special music video.

Musicians as Spokespersons

The California Milk Processing Board has tapped tween musical acts including Britney Spears and Hanson to appear in their milk mustache ad campaign. Reebok has promoted its tween girls shoe offerings with ads featuring Columbian pop singer Shakira.

Opportunities abound for you if you recognize the importance of music to today's tweens and use their music to communicate that your brand is relevant to their lifestyle.

TWEENS AND PLAY

The tween stage is a unique age when kids want to be grown up, but they still cling to the joys and ease of childhood. Marketers to tweens must remember that fun and play are important parts of the lives of individuals in this age group. Product development, advertising, packaging, and especially promotion must strive to keep this in mind.

Play is the work of kids. This has been true forever. Kids go to school, eat, sleep, and play. That's pretty universal. Our parents played marbles in the schoolyard. We played trucks in our bedrooms. Today, kids play with GameBoy on the way to soccer practice. Although the actual activities change, there are certain consistencies in the way kids play.

Kids become tweens, then teens. As they get older, traditional play patterns like collecting, action-playing, and role-playing are cast aside for video games, remote control vehicles, and other electronic items. With regard to play, tweens are in a dynamic period of change where it becomes more difficult to discern kid-like behavior from tween behavior. To help make this distinction, we will discuss tweens in terms of emerging tweens and transitioning tweens.

Let's review three play patterns that are most relevant for tweens.

Collecting

Through time, kids have collected items like marbles, baseball cards, stamps, Beanie Babies, Pokémon, and Yu-Gi-Oh cards. Tweens collect for many reasons. Some want to have an enormous collection they use for play, some want to use their collection as a retirement tool if it is sold, and some just want to use it as social currency.

So, why do most tweens collect? One reason is that tweens love quantity. Their status is often measured by the quantity of every thing they own, whether the number of lipsticks or the number of Hot Wheels cars. Collecting can also satisfy more unconscious needs like the motivational needs we talked about earlier in this book—power, freedom, fun, and belonging. Here's how each motivator relates to collecting.

- *Power*—the ability to accomplish
- *Belonging*—the ability to have what others are interested in
- *Freedom*—the actual labor of collecting; the personal aspect
- *Fun*—the thrill of the chase

Let's use the collecting of Pokémon cards as an example.

The Pokémon fantasy is so rich and developed that it became an instant hit in the United States. The cards were highly sought after; there were even reports of card theft and knife attacks among kids. Many schools banned the cards because of the level of distraction they caused. So, how were tweens motivated by Pokémon?

- *Power*—having knowledge over parents. For hours, tweens could carry on detailed discussions about which Pokémon can evolve, which power is dominant, and who is the better trainer. Parents had no clue what was going on and tweens loved it.
- *Belonging*—knowing everything (and hopefully more than everyone else knows) about Pokémon. It was almost like a brotherhood. Everyone spoke the same language.
- *Freedom*—owning the fantasy understood only by Pokémon Masters enabled freedom. Kids could devour play that their siblings might not understand. Tweens could freely trade cards among themselves.
- *Fun*—playing the complex game, savoring the thrill of the chase in collecting all 151 cards, and even in saying their names. It was complete fun!

Over time, the cost of collecting has become higher and higher. Tweens have been able to keep pace with this increase because of the high levels of disposable income they enjoy. Tweens were more than willing to pay $3 to $4 a pack for Pokémon cards to find the elusive Mew or Charizard card. A $7 Beanie Baby is certainly not out of the question.

Some of today's tweens are collecting unopened toys like Starting Lineup figures and Barbie Dolls as well as cards and trinkets. We adults either marvel at the patience and tenacity of kids and tweens collecting unopened toys or we cringe at a seemingly lost childhood. Aren't all toys meant to be played with?

Action Play

Action play is as old as toys themselves. In this play pattern, youths use toys (like action figures, construction toys, and vehicles) to create play. Here, the child takes on a central role that completely controls the play sequence. Some call it the "God complex." Basically, for all the toys (characters) involved, the child determines the plot, delivers all dialogue, and controls all destinies.

Action play is a far more friendly play pattern to tweens than collecting or role-playing. Not only is it the most common type of play pattern and therefore the most enduring, but this play pattern is also empowering. One of the most popular toy brands ever developed was Power Rangers. In 2003, 14 years after its introduction, Power Rangers was still a $125 million a year brand. The key to its success rests not only in the brand's annual rebranding or in entertainment alliances, but in how the fantasy meets all the motivational triggers for kids.

Toy manufacturers are trying to maintain tween interest as long as possible by injecting electronic components into the toy aisle. They are trying to make toys as relevant as possible to an audience that craves innovation and is accustomed to being entertained. Now, action figures can download data or speech from TV shows as they air, giving new life to action figure play. Action figures also are being created under licenses that come from movies or video games, further spurring interest from the tween group.

Role Play

Role play is the oldest known play pattern, but it is waning in popularity, as today's youths become more mature earlier in their lives. Role-play is very empowering because it allows kids and young tweens to transform into someone else. They become Luke Skywalker or embody "the teacher." Sometimes the simplest "props" can help transform a persona. Pistols made from the index finger and thumb have held up more villains than we'll ever know.

"Role play seems to be less imaginative now than in years past," says Kate Gearding, former toy marketer and youth marketing consultant for WonderGroup. "Toy manufacturers provide more realistic props and kits for creating role-play. For instance, when my brother played Darth Vader, his light saber was a stick. Now, you can buy light sabers that light up, retract, and make noise as they slice through the air and make contact. Computerized cash registers take the "ch-ching" out of make-believe grocery store encounters."

With the popularity of electronics and video games skyrocketing, parents are left to wonder about the impact it will have on their children. Certainly one symptom is that imaginative play patterns such as role-play suffer most.

Interactive Toys and Video Gaming

Over the past few years, toys are more contrived and have become less imaginative. Throughout the past 20 years or so, the top five best-selling nonpreschool toys (excluding video games) were generally action figures, Barbie and other dolls, and occasionally a Hot Wheels car assortment. In 1997, electronic, interactive toys such as Tamagachi Pets,

Giga Pets, and later Furbies broke into the top five selling toys. In 2002, Hasbro's FurReal Friends evolved the concept of a robotic pet with life-like fur and movement. It was a realistic, purring, cuddly kitten that caught the fancy of kids and tweens everywhere. Hasbro also made Karaoke electronic singing machines that became all the rage. For perspective, a list of the top five selling toys each year is shown below.

Added to this move towards reality and fantasy-based toys is the continued growth of video games. New and updated versions of popular gaming systems now allow players to participate in even more realistically performing video games systems. The systems that have become synonymous with video games are: PlayStation 2, the Nintendo Game-Cube, Microsoft's X-Box, and the GameBoy Advance.

Tweens, especially boys, love their video games. On average, tweens play video games for 47 minutes a day—50 percent more time than reported for teens and more than 250 percent of the time reported for younger kids. More than 80 percent of tweens grow up in households possessing video game units, and 47 percent of today's tweens have video game units in their bedrooms.

FIGURE 8.4

Top Five Selling Nonpreschool Toys

1994	1995	1996
Power Rangers	Barbie Sister Kelly	Holiday Barbie
Power Ranger Karate	Sky Dancers	Star Wars Figures
Home Alone Talk Boy	Batman Figures	Hot Wheels 5 Car
Bedtime Barbie	Barbie Stroll Set	Barbie House
Gymnast Barbie	Teacher Barbie	Pet Doctor Barbie
1997	1998	1999
Tamagotchi Pets	Hot Wheels Basic	Furby
Holiday Barbie	Spice Girl Dolls	Hot Wheels Basic
Giga Pets	Holiday Barbie	Star Wars Assorted 1
Star Wars 1	Furby Assorted	Barbie Millennium
Star Wars II	Hot Wheels 5 Car	Pokémon Cards
2000	2001	2002
Hot Wheels Basic	Hot Wheels	Barbie Karaoke
Poo-Chi Robot Dog	Rumble Robots	Bratz Dolls
Barbie Crusin' Jeep	Barbie Crusin' Jeep	Cranium Board Game
Tekno Robot Dog	Barbie VW Beatle	Hot Wheels
Celebration Barbie	Barbie Karaoke	Karaoke Machine & Monitor

Source: Toy Manufacturers of America

Generally, the move towards greater reality in toys together with increased use of personal computers, Internet, and video games points to a significant reduction in the amount of time today's tweens spend using and exercising their imaginations. Where this will lead will be interesting to observe.

Play by Years

Another look at how kids change as they become emerging tweens and then transitioning tweens can be seen by observing the toys they play with.

Prior to the holiday season of 2000, we asked 550 kids and tweens for their "wish lists" in order to better discern how play changes as young kids become tweens. A list of their top choices by age is shown at right and below.

KIDS & TWEENS FAVORITE TOY "WISH LIST" BY AGE

Boys

Age by Year			
6	Video Games	Scooters	
7	Video Games	Legos	Robotic Dogs
8	Video Games	GameBoys	Video Game Systems
9	Video Games	Scooters	Video Game Systems
10	Video Games	Video Game Systems	Scooters
11	Video Games	Video Game Systems	Scooters
12	Video Games	Scooters	Video Game Systems
13	Video Games	Video Game Systems	Cash $/Blades

Girls

Age by Year			
6	Baby	Dolls	Barbie
7	Barbie	Baby Dolls	Robotic Dogs
8	Barbie	Baby Dolls	Scooters
9	Barbie	Scooters	Assorted Dolls
10	CDs	Clothing	Scooters
11	CDs	Jewelry	Barbie
12	Jewelry	Clothing	CDs
13	Clothing	CDs	Cash $

Source: Wish List Study, WonderGroup, Inc.

SOME OBSERVATIONS

When it comes to boys, video games rule throughout the kid and tween years, whether among 6 year olds or 13 year olds. In fact, video games and video game systems were one of the top two choices of one out of every three boys. Also as expected, scooters were the hot new outdoor activity for the year.

When it comes to girls, Barbies and baby dolls rule until the age of 10. Then clothing, jewelry, and CDs take over. Here again we see clear evidence of the emerging tween.

Over the years, there has been quite a bit of speculation regarding the "closet kid" inside of every tween. Among their friends, tweens may exhibit disdain for playing with toys from their younger years. However, secretly, in their rooms, girls may like to play with dolls occasionally, while boys may play with their trucks or trains. This is not surprising because they are still children in some ways. Our wish lists found some evidence of this. For example, among boys we found that while requests for basic-type of toys, such as Legos, remote control vehicles, stuffed animals, and toy-based games trended downward as kids became tweens. Yet, more than 80 percent still requested basic toys in their early tweens. For boys, the big disinterest in these types of items seems to occur as they become very late transitioning tweens to early teens.

Not surprisingly, we see tween girls leaving traditional play and toy items at an earlier age than boys. However, we see that about one-quarter of tween girls aged 10 and 11, still request Barbie dolls. We cannot be certain as to whether the Barbie requests had to do with play desires or, rather desires to "collect." As for requests for items like baby dolls, these seem to erode steadily throughout childhood and virtually disappear as the girls become transitioning tweens.

THE "CLOSET KID" INSIDE EVERY TWEEN REQUESTS FOR BASIC TOYS BY AGE

Boys

Age by Year	
6	97%
7	84
8	84
9	61
10	57
11	57
12	39
13	11

Girls

Age by Year	Barbie Dolls	Other/ Baby Dolls
6	19%	62%
7	52	42
8	53	30
9	28	24
10	28	24
11	28	8
12	12	8

Source: Wish List Study, WonderGroup, Inc.

MARKETING, ADVERTISING, AND NEW PRODUCT DEVELOPMENT

9

THE OLD MEDIA AND
THE NEW MEDIA

Hundreds of empirical studies conducted over the past 50 years leave little doubt that kids' beliefs, attitudes, and behavior can be greatly influenced by exposure to media content. With the many new introductions and changes recently witnessed in the kid-media arena, it is no wonder that we see children developing and acting differently than tweens of just a few years ago.

PERCENT OF 8 TO 13 YEAR-OLDS WHO LIVE IN HOMES WITH . . .	
TV	99%
VCR	97
Radio	96
Tape player	96
CD player	92
Computer	83*
Video game player	82
Cable TV	74
Internet	65*
CD-ROM	58
Premium cable	49

Source: Kids & Media: The New Millennium, Kaiser Family Foundation, November 1999
*Updated statistics from Grunwald Associates, 2003

THE NEW MEDIA LANDSCAPE

Today's tweens live in the most media-rich environment in history. The typical tween lives in a house with three television sets, two VCRs, three radios, three tape players, two CD players, a video game player, and a computer. Over one-half of all tweens' homes are connected to the Internet, according to information from Grunwald Associates.

Things have certainly changed since the pre-TV years when parents were able to exert control over their kids' access to

PERCENTAGE OF TWEENS OWNING DEVICE THEMSELVES

CD player	72%
Radio	71
Television	62
VCR	50
DVD player	38
Internet	20
Telephone	11
Computer	9
Digital camera	7
PDA	6
Cellular phone	6
MP3 player	3

Source: WonderGroup/KidzEyes 2003 Survey

AVERAGE AMOUNT OF DAILY MEDIA EXPOSURE BY YOUTH SEGMENTS

2 to 7 years	4 hours, 17 minutes
8 to 13 years	8 hours, 8 minutes
14 to 18 years	7 hours, 35 minutes

Source: Kids & Media: The New Millennium, Kaiser Family Foundation, November 1999

commercial messages. Before the prevalence of television, children were about age 8 (the age of today's tween) before they could access messages on their own because they could not read competently until then. Their parents (especially their moms who tended to stay at home) had more than enough time to provide them with the proper guidance needed to interpret the meaning of print. However, with years of exposure to TV, radio, and the Internet, without the control of parents, today's kids have already received and processed years of messages by the time they become tweens.

Today's tweens use more types of media than ever before, and they are more likely to be exposed to it without any adult supervision. In many ways, today's tween bedrooms are mini-media centers. More than one-half of all tweens have televisions, radios, tape players, CD players, and, for boys, video game players, in their bedrooms.

These tweens are exposed to and use more media than any other youth segment, which makes them the easiest of all youth groups for marketers to reach with advertising. The Kaiser Foundation's November 1999 study, Kids and Media, found that tweens expose themselves to more than eight hours of in-home media daily.

Note: These numbers reflect some simultaneous exposure to more than one medium at a time and also include both advertising and non-advertising-based media, such as TV, taped shows, videotapes, movies, video games, print, radio, CDs, tapes, and computer.

TELEVISION IS KING

Despite the introduction of new media, such as videogames and the Internet, television is still by far the king of media vehicles for reaching this market. As shown in Figure 9.1, television accounts for more than

OTHER POPULAR SHOWS TWEENS WATCH

	Percent of 8 to 11 Year-Olds Who Watched in the Last 7 Days	Percent of Show's Total Audience Who Are Aged 8 to 11
SpongeBob Square Pants	56.9%	69.3%
Rugrats	55.6	65.3
RocketPower	52.9	73.9
Scooby Doo	52.3	65.7
Dexter's Laboratory	50.9	69.6
Fairly Odd Parents	45.2	74.7

Source: Simmons Kids Study, 2002

three-quarters of a tween's daily media use. Moreover, while there has been a proliferation in the number of TV channels being broadcast, tweens are still relatively easy to target. Today, tweens can choose among such youth-targeted networks as: Nickelodeon, FoxBox, Kids WB, Disney, ABC Family, Discovery Kids on NBC, ABC Kids Saturday Mornings, Cartoon Network, and, at times, the WB. As they reach their upper tween age, MTV even enters the picture.

Targeting just a few shows can reach a large share of the tween population. According to the 2002 Simmons Kids Study, 55.6 percent of 8 to 11 year olds report watching *Rugrats*. In addition, tweens represent 65.3 of all kids (aged 6 to 11) watching this show.

Tweens favorite TV viewing runs the full gamut of drama, movies, music videos, sports, news, animation, comedy, and children's entertainment.

FIGURE 9.1
Tweens' Average Daily Exposure to Advertising-Sponsored Media

Excludes non-sponsored media—videotapes, movies, video games, CDs, tapes

	Amount of media use Hours:Minutes
Television	3:54
Shows	3:37
Taped shows	0:17
Radio	0:35
Print	0:23
Magazines	0:17
Newspapers	0:06
Computer	1:18

Source: RoperASW 2003

Television Tastes

Because tweens are constantly growing away from childhood and towards being teenagers, their favorite TV viewing runs the full gamut of drama, movies, music videos, sports, news, animation, comedy, and children's entertainment. Boys and girls show different preferences, particularly with action/adventure, music videos, sitcoms, and sports.

A May 2000 *Sports Illustrated for Kids* Omnibus Study found that when it comes to tween's favorite TV shows, comedy and

KIDS' REPORT FAVORITE KINDS OF TV SHOWS

Genre	Boys 9 to 11	Girls 9 to 11
Cartoons	81%	72%
Comedy	35	44
Action/ Adventure	44	18
Nature/Animal	25	28
Music Videos	10	24
Sitcoms	14	26
Sports	24	5
Reality Shows	11	14

Source: C&R Research

animation share the top spot for those aged 9 to 11. No longer are *Full House, Fresh Prince, Martin,* and *Home Improvement* around to garner favorite votes for comedy. Instead, in 2002, shows such as *Fairly OddParents, 7th Heaven,* and *Survivor* are among tween favorites in animation, drama, and reality. The Nickelodeon Channel is a favored genre of its own. Since 1995, drama and The Nickelodeon Channel have moved up at the expense of comedy. Animation has made gains as well.

RADIO

There is some discrepancy as to just how much radio tweens listen to. One study, a Kaiser Family Foundation report, found that tweens generally listen to about three hours of radio a week (among younger tweens) and five hours per week (among 10 to 13 year olds). The 1998 Roper Youth Report found tween radio listening to be about five hours weekly. The recently released Arbitron study, How Kids and Tweens Use and Respond to Radio, found just about all kids and tweens (90 percent) tuned into their favorite radio stations eight to nine hours a week.

Radio is a significant media vehicle used by today's tweens.

Although the data do not all agree, radio is a significant media vehicle used by today's tweens. They listen while in their rooms alone at night, using the Internet, reading, and driving to Little League games with a parent.

Unlike other demographic groups, tweens tend to concentrate their listening within a small number of stations, with 80 percent of all listening reportedly going to the station that they listen to most. Tween use of radio generally mimics that of teens, in that tweens favor one type of station. For example, while 62 percent of kids aged 6 to 8 report listening to Radio Disney/kid radio, 72 percent of 9 to 11 year olds report listening to Top-40 stations, according to a Next Generation Radio Study with Arbitron.

PRINT

As children enter their tween years, print becomes a viable media option to reach them. Studies have found that 88 percent of all tweens report reading a kids' magazine at least once over the past six months. As shown in Figure 9.1, tweens spend an average of 17 minutes each day with magazines. That is quite a bit of time to spend with this medium, and it is 20 percent more time per day than the amount reported for teens.

According to *Magazine Dimensions,* there are now some 250 children's magazines, but many are not viable advertising vehicles (small audiences, local editions). Magazines are a viable medium to extend reach among kids, particularly if they come from light-TV viewing households. Simmons' Kids Study measures audience levels for the primary, viable titles: Below is a sample of the excellent magazines developed just for this age group and their readership among tween boys and girls.

In looking at some of the leading magazines read by today's tweens we can see what their appeal is to tween consumers.

MAGAZINE READERSHIP (IN THOUSANDS)		
	Boys	**Girls**
Publication	**8 to 11**	**8 to 11**
Nickelodeon	1,690	1,864
National Geo for Kids*	1,484	1,316
Disney Adventures	994	1,500
Sports Illustrated for Kids	1,748	541
Playstation Magazine	1,030	282
Boy's Life	994	169
Beckett Baseball	761	373
Beckett Baseball Card	647	214
Beckett Football Card	844	258
Humpty Dumpty	332	610
Jack & Jill	461	497

Source: Simmons Kids Study, Spring 2002
*estimated readership reported from National Geographic

- *Disney Adventures.* This magazine covers topics as diverse as entertainment, technology, and real life adventures of fellow kids. The magazine features several games, comics, and puzzles and is written largely for kids in their tween years.

- *Sports Illustrated for Kids.* This magazine uses tweens' love of sports as the hook to engage them in learning. The magazine quietly reinforces history, math, and science lessons. It is used to some extent by educators to assist in their teaching.

- *Nickelodeon.* This magazine prides itself upon creative content. Every issue has a particular theme that follows throughout the course of the issue. Regular features include Ooze News, comics, games, and puzzles.

- *National Geographic for Kids.* Newly launched since 9/11, this highly-branded title has experienced several circulation increases during the first few years of its publication. Kids' interest in international issues significantly increased after September 11, and demand from kids for their own magazine in the current event/international category caused the National Geographic Society to respond to fill the void.

Speaking of filling voids, other magazine spin-offs from adult titles have also appeared with huge success. Although geared toward teens, many of these new magazines, *Teen People, CosmoGirl, TeenVogue,* and *Elle-Girl,* have filled a huge fashion and pop-culture void particularly among girls. Older tween girls have always read teen titles, but these new magazines have experienced huge success, partly from tweens moving into the fashion category at earlier ages.

Print allows marketers to reach a significant percentage of the total tween audience. Considering "pass along" rates, a magazine such as *Disney Adventures* reaches almost 20 percent of all 9 to 11 year olds. One ad in *Sports Illustrated for Kids* and *Nickelodeon* each reaches 17 percent. Thus, even if the same kids read more than one magazine, a marketer could reach a significant audience among the tween and kid population for only about $150,000 (one insertion in each of the three magazines).

OUT-OF-HOME

While historically not thought of as an important medium to tweens or kids, outdoor (out-of-home) media is beginning to surface as an interesting addition to the tween marketer's media mix because of the increased mobility of today's tweens and teens.

Tweens go shopping and frequent movie theatres with and without their parents. A favorite pastime is going to the mall "to hang out." This mobility makes them reachable by standard outdoor billboards, in-store advertising (such as floor graphics, shopping cart and bag ads, video-store receipts), mall arcade ads (companies such as Channel M and Video Walls), and other in-mall ads. Procter & Gamble unveiled new Internet-connected kiosks in various malls, allowing tweens to try on Cover Girl products and surf the company Web site. Movie theatres hold an audience captive, and we've all seen how the theatres strive to keep patrons entertained before the movies start with interactive slide presentations and rolling-stock commercials during the movie previews. Theatre sampling, signage, and events add to the entertainment value for tweens who go to the movies often.

While out-of-home media does reach tweens, it is very difficult to target, which is the nature of this medium in general. When using outdoor advertising, marketers usually wind up paying for a much more diverse audience than just tweens. But it has its purpose to gain broad awareness among tweens (and their parents) or provide store location directions for retailers.

When using outdoor advertising, marketers usually wind up paying for a much more diverse audience than just tweens.

NEW MEDIA

Possibly the one thing that makes today's tweens different and more powerful than any of their predecessors is their access to, and familiarity with, computer technology. Today's tweens are the first tweens to grow up with computers and the Internet. For the first time ever, tweens have the power to access information as fast and as easily as their curiosity demands.

Access to almost unlimited information, combined with the unbelievable curiosity that kids possess, makes this media truly capable of changing the way tweens will learn, become adults, and become tomorrow's consumers.

As we know, all kids are curious. Because they never know what they'll see, they will always look. Now, imagine the potential of bringing this boundless curiosity to a vehicle that allows you to learn and explore in the quickest, easiest ways imaginable—the computer and the Internet.

Of today's tweens, 83 percent report using a computer at home at least one hour per day. Nearly half of kids who go online at home have a computer designated for their use alone (mom and dad have their own computer). Tweens go online an average of four days a week.

While tweens use computers for a variety of tasks, the number one reason is playing games. Tweens spend more time on computer games than on any other recreational use of the computer. Boys say that they spend just over twice the amount of time playing computer games as they spend on the computer doing school work. For girls, the two computer activities are about equal.

TWEEN COMPUTER USE

Percentage of tweens aged 8 to 11 reporting using a

Computer	95.6%
At home	83.3
At school	86.6

Source: Simmons Kids Fall 2003

FIGURE 9.2

Online Activities: Percentage of Kids Saying They Engage "Very or Pretty" Often

	ALL KIDS	KIDS 9–11	ALL BOYS	ALL GIRLS
Send or receive e-mail	75	57	65	84
Use Instant Message	56	32	50	63
Play Games	54	71	56	52
Listen to music online	54	26	35	41
Download music	39	11	38	30
Do homework	32	33	31	33
Get info about movies	27	21	25	30
Get current news/info	27	22	28	27
Visit chat rooms	23	22	15	20
Buy things	11	8	11	10

Source: RoperASW 2003

About one-half of all tweens use the Internet, and this is not just done in the school but mostly at home. Almost three-fourths (72.1 percent) of tweens using the Internet say that they do so from their home. This compares with only 47 percent reporting Internet usage from school. In addition, while gaming is an important reason for using the net, other reasons surface as well.

As tweens age upwards, their time on the Internet grows, perhaps because they are likely to be at home alone more often. Specifically, our WonderGroup/KidzEyes 2003 study found that online tweens aged 10 to 12 spent a little more than twice the time on the Internet as 8 and 9 year olds.

No matter what the age, both emerging and transitioning tweens spend the majority of their time (61 percent) on the Internet sending e-mail or chatting. In fact, tweens aged 10 to 12 (who spend about one hour a day on the Internet) reportedly spent almost one-half hour every day just chatting on line.

Web site and search engine visitations among tweens has increased lately, with 69 percent of tweens aged 8 to 11 reporting they visited a Web site or search engine in the past month, according to Simmons Kids 2003 study.

WHERE TWEENS USE THE INTERNET	
Home	72%
School	47
Friend's home	24
Library	11

Source: Sports Illustrated for Kids Omnibus Study Wave I&II, February and May 2000

WHY TWEENS USE THE INTERNET	
Games	71%
E-mail	57
School work	33
Chat (IM)	32
Information on music	30

Source: RoperASW 2002

**TYPES OF WEB SITES
TWEENS VISIT**

Share of kids aged 8 to 13 visiting each type of site the previous day (among those visiting any site).

Entertainment	46%
Gaming	31
Sports	18
Research/Information	13
Shopping	10
Relationship/lifestyle	8
Search Engines	8
Family/Children	7
News	7

Source: WonderGroup/KidzEyes, December 2000

If you are going to advertise on a Web site, there are a few that seem to generate an impressive number of visits. Specifically, our December KidzEyes panel found two-thirds of all tweens on the net report having at least one favorite Web site.

When asked for their one most favorite Web site, our panel split among literally hundreds of different sites. The most heavily trafficked sites vary depending on product promotion activity. Neopets.com has consistently been in the top-viewed list due to keen interest in the NeoPets product line, and Mattel had a lot of traffic for a while due to Diva Starz and Barbie promotions. Other sites heavily frequented by tweens, consistently, include Disney.com, Nick.com, Yahooligans, AOL and AOL Instant Messaging, Cartoon Network, and Amazon.com.

Consistent with their primary reason for using computers and the Internet, those who visit Web sites reported doing so more for entertainment reasons than for school or research. According to our December KidzEyes panel, a big reason for choosing a Web site as their favorite was gaming.

It is interesting to note, particularly for retail marketers, that one in ten 8 to 13 year olds who visited a site the previous day visited a shop-

FIGURE 9.3

Highest Rated Web Sites by Kids 6 to 14

(Total Universe: 17,443,000 Web Users Age 6 to 14)			
Site	**Unique Audience**	**Target Reach**	**Composition**
AOL	5,774,000	33.1%	12.6%
AOL IM	2,279,000	13.1	19.4
Amazon	2,148,000	12.8	9.7
Disney	1,805,000	10.7	29.2
Ask Jeeves	1,540,000	8.8	17.9
Nick.com	1,314,000	7.5	49.5
Cartoon Network	1,128,000	6.5	49.3
Neopets.com	1,022,000	5.7	54.1
Mattel	869,000	5.0	38.6

Source: Spring 2003 Nick.com/Nielsen/NetRatings

ping site. Not only do some tweens visit shopping sites merely to get an idea of what to buy or ask for, but some are active buyers as well. Clothes, CDs, and various toys such as DragonBall Z figures and Beanie Babies top the lists.

Computer's Effect on Other Media

We can now say that the computer is a strong force in gaining time and attention of today's tweens. There are huge discrepancies, however, across the different research studies concerning exactly how much the computer has affected tweens' interaction with other media. There is a reported decline in TV and video viewing, but not in the same proportion to the increased time spent on the computer. According to parents, the computer has had a favorable impact on their children's reading, listening to music, and other activities.

MULTI-TASKING AND MEDIA

Maybe because their time is so tight, or maybe just because they can do it mentally, today's tween is a media multitasker.

When they are on the computer, they are also likely to be watching TV, listening to radio, and talking on the telephone. In fact, many tweens tell us in focus groups that they and their friends regularly chat online about a TV show they are all watching simultaneously.

**INTERNET IMPACT
ACCORDING TO PARENTS**
Parent's opinion as to change in child's activities since using Internet from home

	Increased	Same	Decreased
Listening to music	32%	62%	6%
Reading books	30	56	14
Time w/friends & family	16	78	6
Watching TV/videos	5	58	37
Reading newspapers/magazines	22	65	10
Using the phone	32	53	13
Making arts & crafts	31	58	6
Playing outside	14	74	11

Source: Grunwald Associates

MULTI-TASKING TWEENS

Things tweens do while on the computer

	Usually	Sometimes	Total
Watch TV	26%	35%	61%
Listen to radio	11	36	47
Talk on phone	8	26	34
Read magazine	4	14	18

Things I do while watching TV

	Usually
Talk on phone	56
Use computer	55
Read magazines	41
Listen to radio	24

Source: WonderGroup/KidzEyes 2003 Study

When you think of it, radio's continued growth as an alternative tween media could well be caused by the fact that it is an excellent multitasking media alternative for computer users. Tweens can easily surf the net or read their magazines while listening to the radio.

While watching their favorite medium—television—several tweens also report listening to the radio, reading, using the computer, and talking on the telephone, all at the same time.

Important for today's TV advertisers is the observation that most often the majority of tweens still just watch TV without doing anything else. TV is still the golden medium for advertising. Specifically, 80 percent of tweens report that they still usually just watch TV without reading, listening, talking, or computing.

IMPLICATIONS

- While computer and Internet usage has impacted greatly on the lives of today's tweens, TV remains the king of the media. Advertising plans should still include this important medium, if you can afford it.
- While TV is the best way in which to reach the most tweens, you can no longer rely on just this one medium to reach all of this audience. Today's tweens are more mobile and highly media fragmented.
- Youth print could make an interesting addition to the media mix, considering that it is read, saved, and shared and the amount of

time that tweens spend with this medium. It is often an inexpensive way to stretch a tight media budget.

- Computer use is becoming a way of life for tweens. Products that make computer use easier, more portable, and more fun will be in high demand.
- Given the small amount of time tweens currently spend on Web sites, companies must develop highly creative interactivity if they wish to motivate tweens to visit their sites.
- If you contemplate the use of Web advertising, consider advertising on or sponsoring the few highly visited tween sites rather than relying solely on your own site or those that are visited less frequently. Of course, advertise your URL in every traditional advertising execution.
- We are likely to see a further increase in the importance of radio as an alternative media for advertising. As computer and Internet use continues to grow, radio may prove an excellent companion media for multitasking tweens.
- Consider Internet advertising in different terms than other reach-oriented advertising (advertising designed to reach the most people a few times, rather than a few people more often). Don't rule out your own Web site which may still be worthwhile for providing tweens with a more complete and deeper relationship with your brand. The challenge will be attracting sufficient numbers of viewers to the site.
- Tweens' tendency for multitasking could make interactive TV and interactive-TV advertising very appropriate for this age group.

10

ADVERTISING THAT WORKS
WITH TWEENS

Among the many consumer segments that manufacturers target with their advertising, tweens may be the perfect audience. For one thing, tweens consume more media than any other youth group. For another, they actually look forward to seeing advertising.

Advertising is the primary source for tween information on new products and, most importantly, for what's cool. Moreover, as tweens get older, many worry about not using the right products and thereby not fitting in with their peer groups. On the most basic level, children want certain products, but tweens feel they need certain products.

Advertising is the primary source for tween information on new products and, most importantly, for what's cool.

A while ago, we had the privilege of helping a client name and market a board game that tested adults' knowledge on advertising trivia, called *Adverteasing*. When introduced, it became one of the country's hottest selling board games, selling well over one million units during its first year.

However, during its first year of marketing, we noticed that most adults had considerable difficulty answering the trivia questions on advertising, and, in some cases, kids were doing much better. That led us to test a kids' version of the game. We will never forget how, when we read some advertising trivia questions to a third grade class. The third graders not only got the answers, but they also got up and literally sang entire advertising jingles. The result was the birth of *Adverteasing Junior,* an advertising trivia board game for kids. *Adverteasing Junior* became an even bigger hit than its adult version.

Lastly, tweens, unlike their younger cousins, "get it." They understand basic messages and story lines of commercials, puns, and exaggerations in print ads. Younger children do not appear to grasp the abstract lessons that are part of some television shows. Significant changes occur, however, around age 7 or 8 when conceptual and symbolic skills develop and mediate TV content. According to Dr. Makana Chock, professor of Children and the Media at Indiana University, children aged 5 to 6 get the basics, but they do not understand time lapses or flashbacks. A young tween will have a better grasp of flashbacks and, by age 11, will even understand irony and sarcasm.

Several years ago, we had the privilege of launching the now famous Super Soaker water gun. We created a funny ad in which a timid boy was harassed by bigger bullies, only to come back as an Arnold Schwartzenegger-type macho man sporting a Super Soaker. The tweens tested loved the advertising spot. They got the humor, loved the story, got the message, and, of course, loved the product. However, when interviewing younger kids (under about age 7), it was like a whole new audience. They loved the commercial, but they loved it simply because it had a big green and yellow water gun.

WHOM TO TARGET, MOM OR TWEEN?

Perhaps the most frequent question we get from marketers is: To whom do we advertise? After all, mom is the purchaser and gatekeeper. Isn't she the primary decision-maker?

Tweens have a heightened interest in products made for them, and they are proficient in "nagging" their parents for these products. For these reasons, we firmly believe it is better to advertise products directly to the tweens instead of, or at the very least, in addition to, their parents.

We firmly believe it is better to advertise products directly to the tweens instead of to their parents.

Too many marketers make the mistake of advertising their tween products solely to moms. Senior managers (themselves, usually older Baby Boomers) often feel uncomfortable in "going-around" moms and advertising directly to tweens. They do not understand that today's moms are very different from those of yesterday, especially when it comes to listening to and even depending upon their children's purchase requests.

PERCENT ADULT PURCHASE RATE IN TEST MARKET AREAS		
	Before	After
Kid TV/Print	1%	9%
Adult & Kid TV/Print	0	4
Adult TV/Print	0	3

Source: 1997–1998 Nag Study

Remember that many parents will not purchase an item for their children unless their child asks for it.

Not surprisingly, Initiative Media's 1997–1998 Nag Study found that parents' awareness and actual purchase of a specific kid product, supported with only a modest ad budget, was highest in markets receiving kid-only TV. In a test-market situation, the kid-only TV test market outperformed adult-only TV and adult/kid-TV markets in all key areas. In fact, the purchase rate actually tripled in the kid-only TV/print market compared with the adult-only TV/print market.

Further, the cost of advertising directly to tweens is far lower than it is to advertise to their parents. This is especially important to marketers whose advertising budgets are at least somewhat constrained. For example, if you wish to reach today's tweens with TV advertising, you could either buy media against the 6-year-old to 12-year-old media demographic or try to buy media against tween moms—women aged 25 to 54. We'll bet that you didn't know that the cost of buying media against women aged 25 to 54 (CPM basis) is 65 percent higher than it is for kids aged 6 to 12. Moreover, more than one-half of those women would not even be mothers of a tween.

The cost of buying media against women aged 25 to 54 (CPM basis) is 65 percent higher than it is for kids aged 6 to 12.

In those rare cases where you do have sufficient funds to advertise tween-used products to the entire family, you can use "all family" TV time to attract both moms and their tweens. In fact, many prime-time TV shows attract more tweens than do typical TV shows on tween-targeted media. However, all-family prime-time TV is far more costly.

When advertising to both moms and tweens, the same commercial can be used effectively providing that you are very careful to make certain that there is an appropriate (usually separate) motivating message to each target. A good example: Sunny Delight has been effective in advertising to both moms and tweens with the same commercial executions. Moms take away the message that Sunny Delight is a healthier beverage alternative that her kids will love. Tweens take away the message that Sunny Delight is a great-tasting, very acceptable beverage that they and their peers like to drink.

Another excellent commercial execution that seems to work for both tweens and moms is the "Where's the cream filling?" campaign for Hostess.

These spots offer humorous situations whereby various animals get into trouble mistaking a truck, trailer, and so forth, for a Hostess cake, only to realize their mistakes by being deprived of the expected "cream filling." Tweens get the humor of these spots and feel that they are the target audience. Adults also get the very same humor and feel the spots work for them. The use of animals instead of human actors brilliantly prohibits viewers from thinking the spot is for someone older or younger than they are.

We will now look at the various opportunities and challenges we face in advertising in each available tween media—television, print, radio, and the Internet.

TELEVISION

The high tween use of television, combined with marketers' ability to target certain TV networks, makes TV advertising the single best way to quickly generate tween awareness. For that reason, we will spend most of this chapter discussing the use of this medium.

When it comes to constructing TV ads for tweens, we are far less constrained creatively than when developing TV ads for younger children. For children aged 7 and younger, you must keep the commercials very simple and straightforward. Young children are quite centric and very product driven. Story lines, humor, and special effects, while fun to create, can actually get in the way when advertising to this group.

TV advertising creatives must avoid techniques such as dream-states, flashbacks, time-lapses, and jumps into the future until the aim is to communicate effectively with tweens and older viewers. Children are much less capable of organizing and integrating story line or plot information until they reach the tween years. Likewise, they do not have the ability to associate events with antecedent and consequent events.

As an example, in 2000, Tyco Toys ran a TV spot for an electric racing car set called Viper. In the commercial, cars must race around the track and try to avoid being snared by a snake head. Some younger children we interviewed thought the ad was about a dinosaur because their own experiences with snakes or vipers were most likely limited. They saw the snake head and not much more.

With tweens as the target, TV ads may use quick-cuts, time-lapses, and humor.

Today's tweens, however, are visually oriented, and, because of their more-developed cognitive abilities, they can react well to significant, rapid, visual changes. With tweens as the target, TV ads may use quick-cuts, time-lapses, and humor. However, if the ad must also communicate to younger children, make certain that these techniques do not get in the way of simply communicating your product to the lower-age group. Remember that this younger group is easily distracted by commercial elements on which you might not wish them to linger.

Moreover, when advertising to young children we must be more constrained in our use of girl talent. The typical rule to follow for ads going to children is "boys will be boys and girls will be either," so it is usually much safer to use boys as the talent in advertising. Young boys just do not want to be thought of as doing things that girls would do. This was again confirmed in a Fall 2000 field exercise conducted by an Indiana University media class assigned to gauge children's response to various TV ads. As Tiffany Ruehl, team captain of the exercise reported, "The younger boys (about age 5 or 6) would sort of just turn away or look down when they saw ads with girls as the main talent. Some actually said things like, 'YUCK. These ads are for girls!'"

It is usually much safer to use boys as the talent in advertising.

However, under certain circumstances, tween spots can safely use either boys or girls, or boys and girls as long as the products and activities shown are relevant to both. For example, we recently showed tween boys a TV spot for a food item in which the primary talent was a girl playing soccer. Boys responded well to the spot. However, when we showed tween boys another spot for this same food item, in which the primary talent was a singing group of girls jumping rope, boys felt uncomfortable with it.

While tweens are accustomed to state-of-the art visual treatments from their computers, Internet sites, and video games, TV commercial production values need not be extravagant. Many marketers make the mistake of trying to compete with the visuals of the more highly produced animated TV shows or video games, and they wind up paying hundreds of thousands of dollars to produce their TV spot. While this certainly does not hurt the spot and may help the marketer or retailer feel that it is a better commercial, it is usually not necessary. Tweens are savvy consumers and want to see the product and what it offers them.

Tweens are savvy consumers and want to see the product and what it offers them.

One of our more successful TV spots to tweens was for a confectionery product called "Sour Brite Crawlers," a gummi worm from the Trolli candy company. The product was a huge success, and research confirmed that tweens literally loved the spot. Its production cost? Less than $100,000.

What Should a Good Tween TV Ad Do?

A January 2001 study conducted among almost 250 tweens by The Geppetto Group, another kids and teens advertising agency, identified the following six pillars of successful tween TV advertising:

1. Getting it
2. Fantasy versus reality
3. Lighter side of teens
4. Showing me the product
5. Music
6. Love, tween style

Getting it. Tweens see advertising as a test of their tentative identities. Being concerned that they are "grown ups" versus "kids," it is important for them to feel that they understand messages that are given to them through advertising. If they do not understand your commercial— or "get it"—they will not blame themselves, but rather blame the commercial. "It is your fault, not mine."

One of the best ways in which to affirm to the tween that they "get it" is through humor.

One of the best ways in which to affirm to the tween that they "get it" is through humor. A good, easy-to-understand joke or situation lets them feel that they are "on the inside." This is a sign that they are growing up.

Fantasy versus reality. Children may live much of their lives in fantasy, but tweens know what they can and cannot do. As such, traditional fantasy takes a backseat in tween advertising because the target audience may think it is too childish. Rejecting fantasy lets tweens reject the child that they do not want to be.

Blending fantasy and reality, while a big challenge, does offer some promising opportunities. Blending fantasy and reality offers tweens a way to understand wish fulfillment or it allows them to make a joke out of reality. It also enables them to feel good about themselves and the commercial because they "get it."

Lighter side of teens. Offering teen life in tween commercials can motivate tweens as long as it highlights the fun, freedom, and confidence of teens, not the more serious sexy, cynical, and rebellious side.

Tweens, especially transitioning tweens, look forward to becoming teens because they perceive this age as having significant advantages.

Tweens perceive teens as having freedom and self-assurance. Teens look better, act better, cope better, and feel better.

Showing me the product. Tweens want to know what you are trying to sell them, what your product is like, and whether it is for them. Make certain that your ad shows your product, what it looks like, how to use it and, equally important, who uses it—namely tweens, like themselves. As Julie Halpin, CEO of The Geppetto Group, reminds us: "Tweens want to see your product, know what it (food) will taste like in their mouths, and what others will think of them when they see them eating it."

Whatever drama or story used in a spot, make sure that it revolves around the product. Paul Kurnit, former president of Griffin Bacal, New York, reminds us that making the product central to the story is part of a larger guideline that is ignored again and again. The product must be the hero.

Music. One of the best ways of letting tweens know your commercial is for them is by the music used in the spot. Remember that music is extremely critical to this age group. Not only do they love it, buy it, and collect it, but they use it to provide themselves with a sense of belonging.

According to tweens interviewed in The Geppetto Group study, music actually ties with humor for the most important element in a tween commercial. The right music can serve as an emotional bridge between the tween and your product. As such, music can move from an ad's background into its foreground.

Love, tween style. While tweens are beginning to become interested in the opposite sex, like their interest in teenagers, they do not want to be reminded of the "uncomfortable" parts of romance. Tween TV spots can show boys and girls together and they can even be sexy. They just can't be sexy together!

Some simple guidelines. What tweens want in a TV spot are the following:

- Kids their own age—if not, then musicians, celebrities, or athletes
- Popular music (radio song, etc).
- Product in use
- Fun, action-packed, happy not scary, romantic

Make the goals of your TV spot simple:

- Communicate the key selling message.
- Create and enforce brand name recall.
- Get tweens to express interest in requesting your product.
- Make it likable (although this is less of a factor).

Test your TV spot before placing significant media dollars behind it.

Test your TV spot before placing significant media dollars behind it. At the very least, show your finished TV spot to a group of tweens to make certain that it is communicating what you want it to. No matter how good your agency is, no matter how many TV spots you might have done for this audience, you cannot view your spot the way a tween does. Many times we have seen a small testing step like this save companies from wasting millions of media dollars by mistakenly placing a very fixable, but uncorrected spot on air.

Just this year we created a TV spot for a toy line aimed at emerging tweens—Blok Bots building blocks that transform into robots and vehicles. We wanted to make 100 percent certain that we effectively communicated the product's name because when looking at the item, tweens automatically and incorrectly thought that it was made by a competitor. To achieve our goal, our creative team came up with a march-like jingle that repeated the name Blok Bots . . . Blok Bots . . . Blok Bots throughout the entire spot. We looked at the finished spot. We loved it. Our client was pleased. Then we tested it among tweens before placing it on air. Good thing! When our tweens saw the test spot, they thought the jingle was saying Black Box, or blah blah. A simple audio remix saved the day. By the way, the product was a big success.

PRINT

As children enter their tween years, print becomes a viable advertising option for reaching this audience. The relatively low cost of media and advertising production associated with print advertising makes this medium an excellent way for marketers with even the tightest of budgets to mount a reasonable national effort to tweens.

As with TV, print ads for tweens can be far more creative than print for younger children. Of course, tweens' reading abilities improve as they age, and they have a far greater understanding of language and use of metaphor. For example in one particular study, children were read a statement like:

> After working there many years, the prison guard became a rock and could not be moved.

When asked about this statement, 5 to 7 year olds thought the guard had physically and magically turned into a rock! The group aged 8 to 9 realized that a physical change did not take place but were still a little confused by the situation. The group aged 11 and 12 got it.

Also, with younger children, print advertisers must take pains to make 100 percent certain that the product and message is extremely apparent in the ad, with virtually nothing else capable of being a distraction from that objective. Unlike tweens, who are much more systematic in looking things over and scanning for the information that they want, children aged 5 and 6 do not scan pictures or print ads but look at things holistically.

Does Print Advertising Work?

Of course it does. Our own research with tweens regarding print has found magazine advertising to be especially effective in extending the recall of advertising in other mediums. Many kids will view a print ad and automatically tell us the selling points of the TV spot they saw for the product. We have even witnessed kids looking at a print ad and automatically tying it together with in-school posters that they saw for the same product.

Many kids will view a print ad and automatically tell us the selling points of the TV spot they saw for the product.

Advertising recall for print is in line with what we would expect from other media for kids. Specifically, in the 1994 Magnet Study, unaided recall for print-advertised kid products ran from 13 percent to 26 percent. Total recall ranged from 51 percent for a candy to 84 percent for a soft drink.

Print offers marketers a few advantages that TV cannot. For one thing, tweens can save your ad. Among kid readers, 83 percent report that they actually refer back to a magazine ad when deciding about a product that they may want. Tweens can also share your ad with a friend. In fact, more than one-third of kid-magazine readers receive their magazine as a pass-along from a friend.

There is a way to have your ad in front of your target every single day of the year, without paying anything more for it.

In some cases, tweens report taping their favorite ads to their bedroom walls. This is especially true if the ad incorporates their favorite sports personality, celebrity, or just an ultra-cool visual. Imagine that! There is a way to have your ad in front of your target every single day of the year, without paying anything more for it. In fact, tweens like certain print ads so much that, according to Michelle Butler of *Disney Adventures* magazine, they will occasionally write to the magazine asking when a certain ad will appear again.

With print ads, tweens can show your ad to their parents making it even easier for them to influence the purchase of your item. Not only can they show their parents exactly what your item looks like, if you have included copy in your ad that can help the tween sell the parent, the tween will use this as well. In fact, 83 percent of kid readers state that they show ads to their parents.

Tweens will spend time interacting with certain print ads, especially if there is a fun, cool contest, intriguing puzzle, or provocative visual. Tweens like to win, and a simple-to-understand contest with the right prizes can get some outstanding results. For example, a simple word puzzle in a Trolli print ad, giving every successful entrant a free bag of candy, generated over 50,000 responses!

What Should a Good Print Ad Do?

The visual is the key. Every time we expose tweens to a sample of print advertising, they are drawn to the most exciting, clearest visuals. The visual should be relevant to the tween, showing his or her favorite sport, fun situation, and so forth. Be careful of inconsistencies and exaggerations. Younger tweens sometimes do not understand a distorted body part or an item doing something or being somewhere it should not be.

If kids are in the ad, their ages, cultures, and overall appearances are of critical importance. As with TV, the talent's age must never be younger than the targeted tween. Remember that tweens do not want to be thought of as "babies," and a younger child in the ad will tell them that this product is for someone younger than they are.

Today's tweens are growing up in a multicultural environment, and they expect advertising to reflect that diversity. A recent study of some print ads for tween girls showed us that this group takes advertising quite seriously. They can be quite critical of the "wrong" type of advertising. For example, we showed 9-year-old to 11-year-old girls some test ads for fashion athletic shoes and were surprised at their dismay over the lack of cultural diversity among the ad's talent. Moreover, when it comes to diversity in ads, tween girls also showed us that it's not only the lack of skin colors that might offend them, but also the lack of hair colors. Make sure your ads show more than just pretty blondes.

As tweens age, they are increasingly concerned about fitting in and wearing and doing the right or cool thing. Therefore talent must not appear to be "uncool" to your audience, or they will assume your product is not for them. In other work we did with tween girls we found them actually projecting themselves and their friends into the print advertising they saw. For example, looking at a group scene of girls hanging out at a slumber party elicited remarks like, "That's me and Katie calling boys on the phone!" or, "This is me and my best friend, Jessica, dancing at a concert." So remember, avoid talent that might project the wrong image and not allow your audience to see themselves in your ad.

While copy can help tweens sell their parents on a specific item, it is far less intriguing to them than visuals. In fact, much of the time, tweens don't read copy at all, even in their favorite ads. Copy should be short and easy to read. It used to be felt that swirly, wavy, or even circled lines of copy would capture the attention of tweens, but lately we have not found this to be true.

In summary, the visual must do it all and tell your essential product story. The great visual captures attention, communicates the message, and involves the product. An ad that relies on a visual to merely capture attention and on copy to make the product connection has to work too hard with this audience. In fact, when your ad is ready to go, ask yourself: "Would a tween want to put this ad on his or her bedroom wall?" If no, try again.

Ask yourself: "Would a tween want to put this ad on his or her bedroom wall?" If no, try again.

RADIO

While radio advertising has traditionally targeted the teen and adult market, it can be a way in which to advertise to tweens as well. This is especially true for products and services less likely to have to need visuals to communicate their advantages. Tweens do listen to radio, especially as they become older. In addition, as we have seen, music is a very important part of their lives.

Radio can be an excellent vehicle for aiding or provoking tween influence because this medium allows marketers to attract tweens together with their parents—especially in cars on the way to and from school, activities, and family outings. According to Arbitron, when it comes to choosing a particular radio station for the family to listen to, in 34 percent of households, the child always makes the choice. In 38 percent of households, the child makes the station choice some of the time.

Among kids aged 9 to 11, 86 percent report actively listening to commercials on the radio. They say they think radio ads are funny and entertaining. Most importantly, the majority of tweens report that radio ads told them about things that they wanted to buy and that they asked someone to buy the item for them.

Although tween use of radio generally mimics that of teens, Rick Berger, president of Next Generation Radio, suggests that it is still very possible to fine-tune ad efforts around tweens. Specifically, tween listening first peaks in the early morning, when tweens are getting ready for school, and then peaks again from 3 P.M. to 6 P.M., right after tweens are home from school. He also suggests surrounding your ad message around "countdown" shows—where the DJ is "counting down" a top-40 list, for example. Lastly, while one might have to buy teen programming in order to reach a tween audience, Mr. Berger states that radio stations will usually work with advertisers to offer rates that would offset any inefficiency that may result.

What Makes Good Tween Radio?

Unlike teens and adults, they are less likely to flip stations to avoid advertising.

The basics for solid tween radio are simple. Make it fun, make it informative, and give it a good musical soundtrack. Remember, unlike teens and adults, this target actually likes to listen to and learn from advertising, and they are less likely to flip stations to avoid advertising.

Concentrate advertising around countdown shows and the peak listening times of before and after school. This strategy allows the best opportunity to capture tweens when they are most likely to be listening to radio.

INTERNET

As tweens continue to migrate to the Internet, opportunities arise for marketers to reach and relate to this target as never before. While banner advertising is becoming less effective as a whole, tweens are more responsive than adults to this form of advertising. Specifically, a recent study found that kids were twice as likely as adults to click through a banner ad. This is especially true if the banner ad offers kids a chance to try new games (the number one reason for visiting Web sites) or get new, free prizes through cool contests.

While the Internet may not represent an efficient way in which to advertise in the traditional sense, it does offer companies an approach to involving consumers with their products. Because of their schooling and overall consumer savvy, traditional passive advertising may no longer be enough to motivate today's tweens. As you will learn in Chapter 12, products must also strive to become a part of tween life through events, school hall-talk, and so on. The Internet allows tweens to become involved with, explore, and learn about products when and where they want to. As such, it plays an important role in overall marketing efforts.

> *The Internet allows tweens to become involved with, explore, and learn about products when and where they want to.*

Companies have designed and marketed Web sites that let tweens play with, listen to, or learn from their brands. As an example, Pepperidge Farm has a Web site that involves tweens with their popular Goldfish Crackers—allowing them to play games using the goldfish as characters. Candystand.com, the highly respected Nabisco site, allows tweens to play games, enter contests, and learn facts about Nabisco's many confectionery products.

Chiquita Brands has long offered a Web site designed to provide retailers and other adults information on its company, brands, and practices. However, realizing that a significant user base for its products is kids and tweens, it developed and offered Chiquita-kids.com, a site offering them games, prizes, sports tips, and, of course, information on Chiquita Bananas.

Other companies have begun to provide their own content to well-trafficked tween sites. For example, some advertisers are profiling their own games and providing animated or live-action characters on Nick.com. General Mills' Cinnamon Toast Crunch has a game, and Mattel used an "adisode" (an episode of an ad) entitled "Dress 'em up and Do the Walk" for its Diva Starz doll.

Other marketers have used the Internet to let tweens learn and experience stories about their products, thus further involving them with the products. As a good example, rather than producing an expensive TV special and placing it on air, Tiger Electronics produced an animated weekly serial comic strip about its new action-figure toy line. Tweens were invited to log on to the Tiger site weekly to catch the continuing story.

Still other marketers promote the "viral" abilities of the Web, constructing and placing Internet ads so entertaining that tweens e-mail them to one another. In a past study that we conducted for a paging product, we asked tweens to tell us about their favorite commercial. In several focus groups held a few years ago in Chicago, the favorite commercial turned out to be for a product that was advertised on the Web through viral marketing—Smart-Beep.

Best of all, the Web can be a terrific tool for marketers to extend their overall advertising effort. Remember that today's tweens are savvy consumers and want to have whatever information they need or want at their fingertips. What better way to offer tweens this than by encouraging them in your TV or print ads to learn more about your product by visiting a Web site? A clothing retailer can feature a great product in its print or TV ads and offer tweens the chance to view its entire line or learn more about fabrics and sizes by visiting its Web site. In various print ads run for Chiquita Bananas, tweens were invited to visit Chiquitakids.com to learn about contests and games. Whenever these ads ran, visitation to the site increased significantly.

What Makes Good Tween Web Sites?

One of the most important factors in effective Web advertising is to make certain that you take steps to attract tweens to your Web message. To do so, you must be aggressive in getting the word out about your site, either through other advertising on TV, in print, or by sponsoring or advertising on the Web site powerhouses frequented by tweens. Many companies make the mistake of sinking significant dollars into developing a wonderful Web site only to find that no one goes there. Remember, there are almost as many sites as there are stars in the sky. While tweens like to use the Internet, they already have their "favorite" sites. Furthermore, on average, tweens spend only a few minutes a day on the Web.

When advertising on the Internet, take special care to be extremely entertaining and encourage viewers to send your message to a friend.

When advertising on the Internet, take special care to be extremely entertaining and encourage viewers to send your message to a friend. Tweens love to share a good laugh or a great commercial. Remember that users are in total control of this medium. If your message is not highly entertaining, they will click off immediately.

If offering a special Web site, make certain that music, action, and fun is used throughout. Today's tweens expect the best. Don't be copy heavy. Tweens want pictures, fun, and action. Copy tends to bore them. As with any other ad, pretest the content and design with tweens to ensure that your site is user friendly.

OTHER GENERAL ADVERTISING GUIDELINES

A few, very important general guidelines to keep in mind when advertising to today's tweens are the following:

- Remember, they are very perceptive consumers. So tell them. Do not sell them.
- Look for ways in which to build the buzz about your product. Add to traditional advertising with appropriate sponsorships, product placements, and merchandising.
- Take pains to ensure that tweens will like your ad. If they like it, they'll watch it repeatedly, paste it on their walls, send it to their friends, and sing its jingle in school hallways.
- Remember that tweens do not share teens' ambivalence about family and its role in their lives. Some ads will do better featuring family environments and situations.
- Remember that nothing rivals the importance and influence of friends to this age group. Show groups of friends when you can.

PROMOTIONS

Promotions, as defined by a standard college advertising textbook, are activities that supplement advertising and personal selling, demonstrations, contests, premiums, and discounts. Are these forms of communication of sufficient interest to tweens to gain attention and possibly drive action? You bet they are!

Years ago, tween-age kids would pester their parents into buying products advertised over the radio during their favorite after-school shows such as Dick Tracy, Terry and the Pirates, Jack Armstrong, or The Shadow. They would use their nag power to get their parents to buy Ovaltine, Wheaties, or other brand sponsors. They would send in the box tops with a nominal amount of money, then eagerly await the prized "decoder ring" or other premium. The makers of Cracker Jack snacks found that offering a "surprise" prize in every box made their product irresistible.

Today's tweens eagerly read the special offers on the back of cereal boxes, and they readily enter contests to win prizes on their favorite Web sites. The main ingredient in promotional strategy for hitting the hot button of tweens is that a promotion brings an element of excitement and fun to the purchase-decision process. As we have discussed many times in this book, the fun element is a strong factor when seeking the attention of tweens. The fact that they get this special treat for little or no additional cost is enjoyed by both tweens and their parents.

Not only do promotions add an element of excitement and fun, but even more importantly, promotions can add an element of news to the product itself. Also, "news" is a very important driver for long-term product success in the youth market. The good news is that kids are often looking to try the next new thing; the bad news is that if your product isn't the next new thing, you'll lose to a competitor! It is not surprising that ad testing service IPSOS-ASI reports that a key determinant of a commercial's success among kids is that the commercial told them something new.

One reason that promotions develop such enthusiastic participation is that today's parents, Boomers and Gen Xers alike, grew up in a period when promotions became part of the marketing mix for many brands. These same parents, who continue to hold onto many aspects of their youth, have passed their enthusiasm for promotions onto their children. Parents receive a sense of gratification when their kids are happy because they won a prize or received an exclusive premium. We have all experienced or read stories of moms and dads gobbling up Beanie Babies at McDonald's for their kids and standing in line at Burger King to get a Pokéball with a prized Pokémon inside. Although most fast-food programs are targeted to younger kids, some promotions such as Beanie Babies and the initial wave of Pokémon fever have hit the mark with tweens as well.

One note of caution for marketers: Pay close attention to how you define who can participate in promotional programs. Many promotions that were specifically targeted to tweens and younger children surprised corporate executives when the grand prize winner turned out to be a 70-year-old grandmother. If possible, try to clearly define the extent of a particular program's legal parameters, the age of qualification for the promotion, i.e., contest winners must be aged 13 or younger.

Two promotional tactics that work well for the tween market are

1. gift with purchases, and
2. contests and sweepstakes.

Gift with Purchases

The word *free* is such a significant word of communication that many marketers have revered it, feared it, and managed to incorporate it into their offering. In most instances it is associated with a guarantee of satisfaction or performance, or it accompanies a promotional offer. For most tweens, the guarantee of product performance, or a free replacement, or your money back, is inconsequential. Tweens assume that the product or service will perform. If it does not, they rely on their parents to straighten it out. They will also never purchase your product again. However, getting something for free along with a product or service they like is something they do understand, something that adds value to the entire purchase proposition, and something that is usually also well received by mom and dad.

The marketers that have embraced the idea of giving a free gift with purchase (also known as giveaways or premiums) to the largest extent represent the Quick Service Restaurant industry, led by market leaders McDonald's and Burger King. Rumor has it that these two companies actually distribute more toys in a year than any of the major toy companies. It is relatively easy to provide a small, exclusive, promotional giveaway with a Happy Meal that pleases a younger kid, but what about the challenging tween?

With concerted efforts directed at gaining the interest of tweens, these and many other companies continually jazz up their product offerings by marketing exclusive promotional giveaways. Many of these promotions center on entertainment licenses.

One restaurant that recently took on that challenge and won big is Pizza Hut. They used an interesting promotion that featured both free products that tweens were interested in (free demos) and a sweepstakes. The promotion was titled "The $500,000 PlayStation/Pizza Hut Giveaway." Featuring a partnership with Sony, Pizza Hut created an instant-win sweepstakes along with a $500,000 grand prize. To get tweens really excited, they layered in a value-added PlayStation demo disc with the five hottest PlayStation titles. Pizza Hut used Crash Bandicoot—a well recognized, edgy property of PlayStation—throughout communications. The results? Four percent sales growth and verified share growth of the target market. In addition, five million PlayStation demo discs were given away, making this a win-win promotion for both Pizza Hut and Sony PlayStation. Rich Matteson, Director of National Marketing and Promotions for Pizza Hut, attributes the success of this promotion to the following four principles:

1. It provided immediate gratification.
2. It was simple and effortless on the part of tweens.
3. It addressed an existing behavior of eating pizza and gaming.
4. Its communications and promotional premium were hip, cool, and trendy.

When dealing with licenses, companies take on big risks for the opportunity of big payoffs (more on this in Chapter 11.) Licensed premium giveaways for Star Wars, Lost in Space, and a number of other movies and television shows sometimes have been received poorly. One restaurant offered the Pokémon characters as premiums six months before they became hot. On the other hand, Burger King had lines waiting out the door at their stores to get the Pokémon items when the time was right. Some entertainment properties allow for promotional opportunities such as actually using the recognizable title characters in commercials.

Recently, more promotions have incorporated music acts. These music acts allow companies to connect with tweens by using live-action commercials of these stars enjoying the company's products. Then a promotional offer for CDs or videos drives action.

Promotions are in no way the exclusive territory of fast-food restaurants. Retailers, entertainment venues, food and beverage companies, fashion manufacturers, school-supply companies, and many other tween marketers have benefited from promotions that offer free or discounted premiums deemed valuable to kids and tweens.

Contests and Sweepstakes

We were recently at a Cub Scout Pinewood Derby in which there were 62 heats. As you might imagine, some of these Scouts and Webelos, aged 8 to 11, were challenged to maintain their focus and interest. But the pack leader organized an activity that kept interest and excitement throughout the night, even for the boys who had lost in the early races and didn't have anything to do but cheer on their friends. The pack had an ongoing raffle or contest in which prizes were distributed based on the number on a ticket given to each scout upon entering the Derby event that evening. In many ways, each tween boy knew he had an equal chance to win something, and he never quit thinking that until the last number was called. Our boys' cars didn't make it past the first round of competition, but they each won door prizes. You would have thought they had won the race by the way they acted when they got home.

The inherent belief of anyone who enters or partakes in a sweepstakes or contest is that they truly have an opportunity to win a valuable prize. Tweens, unlike adults who have more experience with the realities of winning a game of chance, really feel they have a good opportunity to be the winner.

Tweens really feel they have a good opportunity to be the winner.

The best sweepstakes promotions offer something for the tween and something for the parents. Give a tween instant gratification with prizes such as free food, i.e., French fries, cash, a free product, and parents a chance for discounts, or a grand prize such as a family vacation, and you usually have a winning combination.

Chiquita, a WonderGroup client, has an ongoing promotional contest as part of its Web site marketing program. Chiquita realized that a strong draw to foster return Web site visits would be an ongoing monthly sweepstakes that awards great tween prizes. In the past few months, Chiquita has given away Media Play gift certificates, GT BMX bikes and team jerseys, Z scooters, Mega Bloks Xtreme Sports sets, and Sega Dreamcasts. Chiquita's costs for these prizes has been minimal, but the interest and excitement generated by the sweepstakes has been extremely valuable. This example emphasizes that with kids and tweens, a huge or grand prize is usually not as significant as the opportunity to win. Many small, correctly targeted prize offerings are much more exciting than a single destination award. If you can add a vacation trip or other significant award for the parents, all the better.

A FEW PROMOTIONS IMPLICATIONS

- Gift with purchase products should be of a high enough quality that they will not immediately disappoint tweens. They should do what they indicate and offer play or other immediate gratification (i.e., food consumption) value.
- Make entering a sweepstakes or contest easy. We learned this from our own mistake. We asked tweens to take pictures of themselves with a product, write a story, and send it in. Only when the responses started coming in did we realize just how complicated this was. Some entries came in without pictures, some without stories, some without either. The entry process took a long time because kids and parents had to buy the product, take pictures, wait for them to be developed, then write stories, then mail in the entry.

Then we had to sort out all the applications and their missing elements. It was way too complicated and too time consuming.

- Carefully evaluate the risks as well as the opportunities associated with licensing. There are great opportunities with new and established licensed properties from youth-focused networks (Nick, Animal Planet, etc.) as well as movies and music entertainers.
- Identify other tween brands that may offer synergistic cobranding opportunities to generate additional voice as well as efficiencies.
- Offer something to benefit moms or families, in association with great targeted prizes for tweens.

11

HOW TO USE LICENSING

Tweens are concerned about being seen with the right products so they can fit in with their peers. That's why visible branding—prominent logos, characters, and so forth—can be either a big plus or minus to your products. If the logo or character is cool and well accepted, then it can be a big plus for the tween to have it. If, on the other hand, the brand or its logo or character is perceived by tween peers as outdated, uncool, or worse yet, too young, then it is a huge risk to use it on a product aimed at tweens.

Rather than spending millions of dollars to create a desirable logo or character of your own, you can license one. Licensing is a huge business, accounting for more than $70 billion in retail sales just within the United States and Canada alone. Last year, it seemed to us that just about every tween focus group we attended could have been a Nike group. Most of the tween boys sported something with a Nike logo on it.

EXECUTED PROPERLY, LICENSING OFFERS TWEEN MARKETERS BIG OPPORTUNITIES

- *A strong license can make a company's product immediately acceptable to tweens (and others) with little or no up-front spending on brand development.* Generally, depending on the item, you can also reduce marketing support funds normally needed to build demand, such as for advertising and promotion. Just think about how a Nike logo can make mediocre or even unacceptable items more acceptable to tweens. Consider adhesive bandages. Working with a client in this field, we found that use of adhesive bandages among kids dropped off a cliff once they approached the age of emerging tweens. Adhesive bandages were just plain uncool. Worse yet, they were "babyish." Tweens told us that it was far cooler to show their cuts or open wounds rather than wear an adhesive bandage. We then designed a concept of Nike adhesive bandages—simple adhesive bandages sporting the Nike swoosh. We tested them among tweens and *pow!* Not only would tweens wear them if they got hurt, but they would wear them even without cuts or wounds. Now that's a powerful license. For the record, because we could not swing a deal between our client and this licensor, the product line never did see the light of day.

- *A strong license is especially helpful to newer or smaller companies vying for increasingly rare shelf space.* The right license can make your product line instantly credible to your sales force and, even more importantly, to the retailer. For example, one of our craft-supply clients was having significant difficulty securing shelf space for its glue products. It licensed Pokémon and got instant distribution. Another of our clients, a leader in rainwear, tried unsuccessfully to gain distribution of a tween line of products. Even though this line promised TV support, cool designs, packaging, and great pre-research results, the trade still would not bite. This year, this same client has the Harry Potter license, and *pow*—up-front orders and distribution.

- *Licensing can even help a company's stock price.* Again, licenses can bring instant credibility to items—even to a company's perceived equity. Wild swings in one of our client's stock prices occurred in 1998 depending upon who had the Pokémon license.

Licensing can even help a company's stock price.   Naturally, the thought of licensing does present some problems and challenges for marketers as well. Marketers have to come to grips with the fact that the items they offer under a license will be far more dependent on an outside party's property rather than their own brand.

Too often we see companies paying significant amounts for a license and then relegating that license to a minor role in packaging and communication for fear that it will dominate their own brand position. If this is what you are going to do, why bother? If your brand is truly so strong that the license is only secondary to an item's appeal, why pay the bucks for the license in the first place? Your own brand can coexist with a licensed offering. However, you must realize that when buying and offering a license, it is usually for the reason of using the license as the primary reason for being. Your brand name must be secondary in this case.

The issues of cost, control, and, lastly, determining what the most appropriate license would be for your needs are also issues you must face if you want to license. During our years of working with clients and licensors, we have found that both cost and control are negotiable. Generally, licensors will welcome an initial proposal from an interested marketer and then the negotiations begin. Final agreements will include the percentage of sales the licensee will pay, a minimum guarantee of royalties to be paid over a course of time, how much money will be paid in good faith up-front, exclusivity, and renewal rights.

Because both parties want a successful venture, the best agreement is usually one in which the licensee generates the highest level of sales yielding the highest level of royalties for the licensor. Therefore, intended levels of advertising and marketing support will be a factor in establishing the final royalty rate and other terms. Here is one guideline: Royalties customarily range from 2 percent to 7 percent of sales on food items and as much as 5 percent to 15 percent of sales on novelty and other items. It depends in part on the demand for the license and the specific category in which the license will be used.

FINDING THE RIGHT LICENSE

As we said before, if tweens perceive a character or logo as outdated, uncool, or, even worse, too young, then licensing it is a huge risk. Too many times we find clients wanting to place a license on a tween-marketed item but then almost making the terrible mistake of acquiring a license that is way too young for today's tweens.

For example, Disney is a great license as long as you are not interested in attracting tweens. Again, tweens do not want to be perceived as being "babies," and Mickey, Donald, and Goofy just don't add up to being "mature" for tweens. On the other hand, Warner Brothers and their Bugs, Taz, and Scooby Doo characters are OK. Why? Because they have attitude. Also, because tweens perceive them as being older.

Drs. Acuff and Reiher of Youth Market System Consulting have found that characters with rounder, softer features tend to be strongly favored by young children, whereas characters with angular, sharper fea-

Characters with angular, sharper features tend to have more appeal to tweens.

tures tend to have more appeal to tweens and up. This helps to explain why Warner Brothers characters rather than Disney's tend to appeal to tweens.

Because it is risky to rely on a license that could become outdated quickly, it is often advisable to forgo the "hottest" licenses in favor of the more tried and true. Gene Del Vecchio, in his book, *Creating Ever-Cool*, discusses the concept of "evergreen" properties and licenses and the advantages these can bring to marketers. Television shows, magazines, other already existing successful brands, fashion brands, and certain retailers all promise potential licensing opportunities with longer staying power. Movies, music stars, and groups are all riskier, but because they tend to be perceived as "hotter" and "newer," they could be bigger sales and distribution gainers.

There are several ways to stay abreast of what is happening in this area. Several magazines—*Licensing, Kid Screen,* and *License!*—cover the topic. There is LIMA, the International Licensing Industry Merchandisers Association, and there is the annual licensing show. Just be careful. Literally hundreds of new licenses for logos and characters surface every year, and each owner will tell marketers that theirs is the newest, hottest license to own.

IMPLICATIONS

- Licensing could be an effective tween marketing strategy for building rapid tween demand and retail distribution.
- Not all licensing is right—choose yours carefully, making sure of its longevity potential and age appeal.

12

FINDING TWEENS AT THE GRASSROOTS LEVEL

One technique growing in popularity and importance in the advertising and marketing community is "grassroots marketing." Grassroots marketing is a catchall term that describes methods and communications channels that fall outside traditional channels of paid advertising, public relations or publicity, and promotion.

The essence of *grassroots marketing* (and the derivation of the term), is the ability of a brand to reach customers in their natural or everyday environment, meaning that consumers experience the brand in such a way that it is viewed as a natural adjunct to their lifestyles, rather than being intrusive or blatantly commercial. The brand has the opportunity to offer a more personal interaction with the prospective customer because the communication is tailored to the specific interest of the targeted demographic segment. For example, Gatorade sets up a booth at a community's junior soccer tournament. It features relevant soccer posters as well as literature about Gatorade and its positive effect in combating dehydration on the soccer field. It also provides free samples of the product. This would be an opportunity for prospects and customers to have a positive interaction with the brand, in a comfortable and consumer-friendly environment. The brand has more impact and its message is made more relevant by complementing the activity or interest of the target audience.

The essence of grassroots marketing is the ability of a brand to reach customers in their natural or everyday environment.

Grassroots marketing efforts have long been part of the marketing formulas of many specialty brands, and in recent years, this has expanded to larger and more widespread brands. Some of the more common grass-roots marketing methods we will discuss are sampling, destinations, clubs, viral (word-of-mouth), and event sponsorship.

SAMPLING

Getting prospective customers to sample one's products is a common, although expensive, method of introducing a product and hopefully gaining a subsequent purchase. Tweens embrace sampling as a way

Tweens like free things.

to experience new products ranging from new ice cream flavors to Chic-Fil-A employees handing out small samples of their chicken filet on a toothpick. Tweens like free things. In focus groups, we've heard them say, when asked what could make a conceptual product even better, "How about make it free?"

The youth-oriented apparel industry has probably been one of the strongest advocates of product sampling. The industry gives edgy fashion designs to influential urban teens and tweens. It hopes that the trendsetters will adopt the styles and that the broader audience will follow suit.

Sampling opportunities abound today. There are structured programs at amusement parks, youth media and local events, Blockbuster Video, Toys 'R Us, and others. One sampling program that we helped design for the Easter Seals charity is the "Giving Back Pak." For a $2 donation to Easter Seals, tweens get samples of products like Sunsweet Fruitlings, Trolli Gummi Bears, Rice Krispies Treats, SweeTarts, Gladware, Motts Fruitsations, and a Pringles-Pak. The products are contained in a psychedelic gift package so that tweens will know the samples inside are for them and moms will know their tweens will like the products.

DESTINATIONS

Destination marketing programs range from small, mobile, local-venue events to huge fixed-site destinations. When you think of large fixed-site destination marketing programs that support brand efforts, the obvious sites that come to mind include entertainment meccas such as Disneyland and Disney World, and more recently, Lego Land outside of San Diego, California. Some smaller venues such as the Sesame Street

Park, Hershey Park, The Crayola Factory, Kellogg's Cereal City, and the American Girl Café also offer customers an opportunity to experience their favorite brands in unique and memorable ways.

For an 8-year-old girl who has a collection of American Girl dolls and accessories at home, the opportunity to have tea at the American Girl Café in Chicago is a new brand bonding experience. It is incredibly powerful for her to be able to take her special doll to the on-site hospital for repairs, while having tea with other girls and their moms, all of whom have a passion for American Girl dolls. When the next opportunity to request gifts comes along (birthday, holidays), or when deciding to spend her own money, the positive impact of the Café experience will help to bring the desire for more American Girl products to the top of her mind.

One destination we recently had the privilege of visiting is the Ciudad de los Niños in Mexico City. It is a huge facility inside a mall, where everything is kid-sized. Moreover, everything is sponsored. Kids and tweens can learn to make a pizza at a Domino's. They can learn dental hygiene at Johnson & Johnson's dental lab. They can learn to be a pilot in an actual fuselage of an American Airlines jetliner, and more. Wow! What a great way to have companies and brands interface with tweens in a fun, educational way. There are current plans to open similar interactive "Kids' Cities" in selected U.S. cities in joint cooperation with the original in Mexico City.

Most brands do not have the luxury of building or affording a high-profile retail destination, but they can take advantage of the many local and regional events that offer an opportunity for companies to set up destinations within their venues. For example, we recently went to a college football game and, within the stadium complex, had the opportunity to see and touch the Tide NASCAR racecar. Tide has, in essence, established a mobile destination within an environment that has already attracted its desired audience. To the teens and young adults who attended this college game, it was an interesting and interactive way of experiencing the Tide brand.

Brands can take advantage of the many local and regional events that offer an opportunity for companies to set up destinations within their venues.

CLUBS

Nothing seems to be more correlated to the youth driver of belonging than to be a member of a club. The establishment of a "club" signifies a common interest, exclusiveness, and a personal acceptance within the umbrella of club membership. Many brands have had success with club membership concepts, and many brands have tried this concept without success. The club relationship, from the standpoint of a brand, has to offer the customer the following benefits.

The Opportunity for Exclusiveness

This could mean special products available only to club members, special prices or discounts for club members, unique information such as previews of new feature products, or opportunities for interaction with other club members.

An Avenue for Interaction

We have seen many clubs that offer only a one-way interaction. If you sign up, we will mail you a newsletter every once-in-a-while. This form of a relationship does not offer any true opportunity for brand bonding because there is no active participation required after the initial request to be in the club. In many of the more successful clubs today, the Web opens up an affordable channel of communication that can allow for an ongoing interactive relationship between the brand and the customer.

Umbrella of Acceptance

Within the branded product-membership or service-club membership, a customer moves from the point of passive purchaser to a stronger, bonded relationship by joining. In order to join, there must be a sense that the individual will be accepted, and that he or she will be part of an environment that includes others who are similar to them. Many youth-oriented clubs help accomplish this by using terminology in the club names (Burger King Kids Club) to make sure kids, tweens, and teens know the clubs are for them.

Thanks to the Internet, clubs are now easier and less costly to set up. For example, when the brand team of one of our clients, Chiquita, first mentioned that they would like to pursue a club concept, they envisioned a program that would collect names for the club and send club members a newsletter a few times a year.

When we looked closely at the cost of membership acquisition, the cost of membership fulfillment, and the opportunity for impact, we determined that within the available budget we could only support a program with fewer than 5,000 club members. We compared the original strategic charge of the Chiquita club concept with the ideal club offerings of the opportunity for exclusiveness, an avenue for interaction, and acceptance, and we found these things lacking in the Chiquita design.

The initial concept relied on a one-way communication from the brand to club members. In addition, it was expensive to fulfill and manage for such a small number of members. If more than 5,000 people wanted to join, the brand would not have the funds to fulfill membership kits.

Using the Internet, we were able to create a Web site destination that offered kids the positive aspects of the original "clubhouse" concept. This allowed us to use the Internet for communications, a Web site for interaction, giveaways, and contests. Ongoing print advertising and in-store promotions supporting the brand were also used to direct traffic to the Web site, www.chiquitakids.com. This program has allowed Chiquita to reach more than 50 times the number of tweens than the initial newsletter program could have afforded in the first year alone. It has also provided a program that builds a stronger brand relationship with kids, with a broader range of interactive content.

VIRAL OR WORD-OF-MOUTH MARKETING

In his recent book, *The Anatomy of Buzz,* Emanuel Rosen provides detail on the phenomenon of word-of-mouth marketing. This form of marketing, in which one consumer advocates the virtues of your product or service to a friend or acquaintance, carries a one-to-one credibility that is not achievable from more conventional advertising methods.

Rosen explains that one of the most important elements of the word-of-mouth marketing lies in the person or persons he calls "network hubs." The identity of these individuals closely resembles the profile of "influencers," identified by Peter Zollo in *Wise Up to Teens. Influencers* are individuals who are likely to be popular, self-confident leaders who enjoy the fact the others will follow their actions.

For the younger tween set, those who establish an initial influencing force are more likely to be sports figures, older siblings, parents, and advertising messages. However, even among these younger tweens, a peer who adopts fashion or other products signals that a new trend is okay to be picked up by the group. For example, a second grader might have seen tie-dyed fashions on TV, and she may have even seen some older kids wearing them. However, the style is acceptable and desirable only after the first person in her class comes to school wearing a tie-dyed shirt.

In the older tween set, where stronger friendship groups have formed, and more tweens have established social sets, the early adopters who carry leadership qualities know, and are comfortable with, their roles as influencers within their circles. Because of their strong desire to assimilate, and the fear of not fitting-in, word-of-mouth marketing within these groups has a tremendous effect.

An industry that has focused much of its attention toward this type of marketing is the computer gaming industry. By seeding prototypes of games with individuals who are high-end gamers, companies benefit from the word-of-mouth marketing spread by these influencers. Because of the dynamics of word-of-mouth marketing, one individual can exponentially reach hundreds with your message.

Because of the dynamics of word-of-mouth marketing, one individual can exponentially reach hundreds with your message.

Here, as in so many other areas of marketing and communication, the Internet can play a huge part. For one thing, we know that the average tween has at least 17 "buddies" on his or her e-mail, and we have seen tweens with as many as 100 or more. In focus groups, we often hear how tweens love to "talk" on the Internet as soon as they get home from school. This talking involves both the sending and forwarding of e-mail and joining in ongoing chats.

Companies sometimes "seed" chat rooms with their own paid representatives in order to begin spreading word-of-mouth interest through the Internet. For example, in return for free CDs and other merchandise, tweens have been willing and eager to join various chats and "spread the word" about certain hot new groups they have "heard."

EVENT SPONSORSHIP

Event marketing has become a growing grassroots marketing method for the tween segment because of the convergence of demographic and cultural trends. The specific and unique tastes and preferences of this demographic group, including a high demand for entertainment, have led to the creation of numerous performance events and groups targeted specifically to tweens. Furthermore, the interest this group has in hands-on and interactive experiences is creating a plethora of opportunities for marketers in all industry sectors.

SFX, the largest and most diversified live-entertainment promoter, quotes a Native American proverb in its promotional literature:

Tell me, and I'll forget. Show me, and I may not remember. Involve me, and I'll understand.

The marketing corollary could be: "Reach me, involve me, motivate me, and I'll buy."

Today's parents seem much more willing to bring their tweens along with them to adult or teen-directed events. Examples of this are events staged by the World Wrestling Entertainment, NASCAR, and concerts by many popular musicians. At a recent sold-out Dixie Chicks concert, there were an amazingly large number of tween girls dressed in chic western wear accompanying their mothers, also wearing chic western wear. During the American Idols concert tour, large numbers of tweens and their parents attended together and experienced first hand the phenomenon which had initially been shared as a family event in front of the television.

Events that target or appeal to the tween segment range from the *Sports Illustrated for Kids* tour, the X-Games, and the Gravity Games, to purely local sports. Entertainment companies have created entire programs targeted to tweens and their parents.

Deciding on the Best Sponsorship

Because there are so many events and so many sponsorship opportunities, it can be difficult to determine the best vehicle for promoting your product or brand. To be truly successful it is critical to select the best opportunities, leverage the maximum from each, and integrate them into an overall marketing program or plan. First, set clear goals for what you are trying to accomplish. Who are you trying to reach? How many of them? What impression are you trying to make? What messages are you sending? What results do you want to achieve?

Nickelodeon Media's All That and More tour stopped at 40 of the nation's largest cities and offer entertainment, music, and opportunities for kids to interact with multiple products and brands. There are many levels of sponsorship. First are the lead or title sponsorships, next are secondary or associate level sponsorships. Because the cost of the top sponsorships can reach $1 million or more, careful selection and management of the sponsorship level and associated program is essential.

There is a common misconception that grassroots events and sponsorships offer a low-cost approach to marketing.

There is a common misconception that grassroots events and sponsorships offer a low-cost approach to marketing. In fact, when done well and on a large scale, these programs are relatively expensive. For example, on the All That and More tour, title-sponsor level with fully integrated promotions and dedicated staffing at each venue could run more than $2 million. With an estimated 440,000 attendees, the cost per kid is $4.50. While this cost may seem high, the ability to interact directly with your brand and attract the right new customers may make it well worth the effort.

Kellogg's Pop Tart brand has tapped into music concert tour sponsorships as one of its most visible grassroots strategies. In the summer of 2001, Pop Tarts sponsored the Aaron Carter concert tour to create awareness and trial of its new Chocolate Chip Pop Tarts. Pop Tarts called on event specialist, Eventive Marketing, to create an 18-foot climbing wall, shaped like a giant Chocolate Chip Pop Tart, which was highly visible at each concert venue. Kids could climb the Pop Tart wall, providing a sense of accomplishment, while their parents looked on. This gave tweens the ability to experience the Pop Tart brand in a new and exciting way, within a very fun environment. A large group lined up at each show in order to participate, and an even larger group watched the action with

interest. Additional elements included signage throughout the venue, product sampling, and a sticker that read, "I Climbed the World's Largest Chocolate Chip Pop Tart." The Aaron Carter tour provided interaction for the brand and its target audience at 46 concert events, with exposure to approximately 250,000 families. Since then, the Pop Tarts wall has been to ski resorts and is now used primarily as a menu activity for retailers and retailer-sponsored events.

In the fall of 2002, Pop Tarts again used concert sponsorship as a marketing tool by sponsoring the American Idols Tour. This followed on the heels of the tremendously popular television program that was the highest rated prime-time television show for both parents and their kids. The sponsorship provided for signage and marquee recognition at events, sampling, and prize giveaways while kids were in line to enter the concert venues. This sponsorship included 26 concert events and reached 150,000 young consumers and family members. By creating an interactive experience with its products, Kellogg's Pop Tarts created great excitement for the brand.

A different type of event and sponsorship opportunity is the Nickelodeon Kid's Choice awards program. This is a once-per-year event that takes place at the Hollywood Bowl with about 11,000 attendees. However, there is a huge television audience for both the live broadcast and the numerous reruns. There is also extensive media coverage of the event itself along with the winners. Therefore, the actual audience numbers in the millions. This property is a closely held asset that Nickelodeon offers to its top advertisers such as Burger King.

Sponsors who take one of the four sponsorships for this event can spend $2.5 million to $3 million in a media buy. This amounts to $1 million to $1.5 million over what might be spent on a traditional media buy. The key to success here is how the sponsor can leverage the event to drive additional business. For any company considering participation or sponsorship of an event such as this, a few words of caution are in order.

Be careful negotiating the rights and privileges associated with sponsorship. Event-related promotions include many legal constraints. For all the right reasons, top kid entertainment producers such as Nickelodeon are very cognizant of staying well within legal boundaries. For example, a gift with purchase that requires kids to buy your product to get the gift can be illegal, or within a legal gray area. A better way to structure a program is to offer a gift for "trying," sampling, or reviewing a product, instead of purchasing.

Be careful negotiating the rights and privileges associated with sponsorship.

Reebok ran such a program with Sears. It offered a free premium seat to the Disney PremEars in the Park show just for trying on its Traxstar sneakers. Obviously, the intent is to spur purchases and gain new customers or incremental sales. An incentive to sample is a first step towards those goals, and is a softer, less aggressive approach that can work well with tweens and their parents.

Another important consideration when negotiating premium-event sponsorships is learning what other sponsors have negotiated as exclusives that might bar your participation. For example, at the Kid's Choice Awards, Burger King executes an excellent promotion where kids vote at the restaurant for their favorite star. This drives traffic to the restaurants. The success of this program ensures that Burger King continues to take advantage of it year after year. No other sponsor is able to offer on-site voting relating to the Kid's Choice awards.

Be on guard against "sponsorship cloning." No matter what organizers say, only one sponsor can truly dominate an event. Some event organizers are so successful at creating "gold" level sponsorships that they then create a higher or "platinum" level. The sponsor who has bought what it thought was a top-level sponsorship could be surprised when a higher tier is created. Alternately, an event owner may create a duplicate premium sponsorship level creating a second gold, platinum, or similarly named level. Of course this pleases the event organizers, but it diminishes the value of each of the top sponsors. Make sure you know what you're getting and that the goalposts don't keep moving after you have signed.

In summary, sponsorship of events is an attractive way for tween marketers to create a hands-on brand experience for a large audience, albeit at a not-insignificant expense. As the previously cited examples demonstrate, choosing the right event and using it in the best way to leverage your brand can be challenging. There are many other events to consider. A few that target kids and tweens include the following:

- American Idol tour
- SFX national music tours targeting teens and tweens
- Harlem Globetrotters World tour
- Sports Profiles Mall tour
- *Sports Illustrated for Kids* tour
- Radio Disney World Radio tour
- Limited Too's Passion for Fashion mall tour
- Disney On Ice tours

Events present an opportunity for marketers to interact directly and face-to-face with tween customers and prospects. The effect that active, three-dimensional promotion has upon customers is significantly higher than that of the relatively passive mediums of television and print advertising. Therefore, you have to measure the cost per thousand impressions (or other measurement) and balance that against the level of impact the impression has. Events can bring your message alive and leverage all aspects of a promotional program.

Evaluating Opportunities

There are three criteria to apply when evaluating an event sponsorship opportunity: synergy, visibility, and scale.

Synergy. As you look at a sponsorship opportunity, first look at the event and its positioning. Does the positioning match your desired product positioning? Once you have determined that the particular event matches your desired brand positioning, the next task is to gauge the true demographic segment that will attend. This is where you need to get some independent advice. Remember that those who sell and present these tours are very polished and can lead you to believe that the tour attracts just the demographic group you want. Ask for independent research on the attendees, and ask to speak directly with previous sponsors, those that resigned and some that did not.

An example of this is the Reebok Traxtar, the first-ever computerized shoe for kids. It shows kids how fast they run and how high they jump. The product was a huge success in the market, becoming the top-

selling kids' shoe in its category and establishing a new higher price point. A big part of that success was getting kids to experience the product in a fun, hands-on environment. In its first year, more than 100,000 kids got to try on the product during national tours and events. This level of interaction with the brand was a critical element leading to the brand's market success.

For Reebok, selecting the right venue for the brand was paramount. Reebok selected the *Sports Illustrated for Kids* tour as a perfect brand fit for Reebok Traxtar. The tour positioned new technology for sports and targeted young tweens with an emphasis on boys, an important audience. Another event used for the same product promotion was The Disney PremEars in the Park Tour.

Part of synergy is getting what you pay for in terms of the target demographic group. In the case of tightly focused segments, this can be a challenge. If you are targeting the female tween segment, aged 8 to 12, often you end up paying for a teen audience as well, making it a more expensive proposition and possibly diluting your message.

Visibility. Visibility is critical. There are two main points to consider. First is the level of overall visibility of the event itself, and second is your level of visibility as a sponsor.

In the first case, you need to look at the event's overall promotional plan and budget. Can this level of expenditure get the visibility and attract the desired audience in the numbers you are expecting? How hot is the lead draw? Will the tour sell out? What is the expected number of tour attendees? This is hard to evaluate and is especially difficult for first-time tours or events.

Getting an in-person audience requires great skill. It is preferable to work with experienced show producers and with tours that have a record of bringing in an audience over a few years. Be very careful with producers who say that most of the tour promotion will be public relations and that most of the audience will be repeat visitors. Look for hard media dollars to promote the event, and evaluate the event promotion plan carefully. There is a distinct advantage to tours sponsored by media companies such as Disney and Nickelodeon because they have access to the TV, radio, and print channels to promote the event at little or no direct cost to them.

There is a distinct advantage to tours sponsored by media companies.

The second point on visibility is whether you, as a sponsor, can break out your brand message in a meaningful way. If you asked a group of tweens who was lead sponsor of the *NSync tour, how many would say

Clairol Herbal Essences? Of course, a big part of a sponsorship rests on the sponsor's ability to leverage the asset in question to drive product awareness and sales. You cannot expect the concert producers to figure this out for you, although they can help on what has worked well for past clients and what is likely to be acceptable to the talent. In this case, Clairol added an outstanding promotion on the back end of the tour. A contest encouraged kids to send in a video of themselves performing their favorite *NSync song. The winners got to have *NSync perform at their school, making the winners true heroes at their school. In addition, public relations from this promotion gained national coverage. In order to get coverage, a promotion needs to be unique and compelling. It is very easy to get lost under the hype for the actual talent themselves.

One critical aspect of sponsorship related to visibility is the optimum level of sponsorship to pursue. In most cases there are title, or presenting, sponsorships and associate sponsorships. Sometimes these levels are called Platinum, Gold, and Silver. What you get from these different levels is hugely different. In principal, we tend to recommend only the top level because other levels offer such low visibility as to make them barely worthwhile.

Part of the success of a sponsorship derives from having clear and realistic goals for the program. The event sponsorship can be part of a larger program leading to prebrand and postbrand awareness. A good example of this is the promotion Reebok ran with Sears for the Disney PremEars in the Park tour. This event previews a new Disney movie and provides entertainment with music and a live stage act with the Disney characters. As a lead sponsor, Reebok set up a promotion at Sears, in which a kid trying on Traxtar sneakers received two premium seats for the Disney event. Sears merchandised the event with in-store signage, special product displays, and so on. The program was a big success for all parties, not only from the perspective of achieving the sell-through targets for the product—a success for Reebok—but by also driving new customer traffic to Sears. Whether people bought the shoes was not a primary concern for Sears. The main point was that Reebok was able to get traffic into its stores. In the retail business, this is highly valued from any vendor.

A quick rule of thumb is to plan to spend at least as much on building an integrated promotional program as you do on the sponsorship.

Many companies under budget for event marketing. Frequently, the entire budget is allocated for the cost of the sponsorship alone. This is a big mistake. In order to leverage your sponsorship dollars, a quick rule of thumb is to plan to spend at least as much on building an integrated promotional program as you do on the sponsorship. The budget should include dedicated staffing, additional tour costs, dedicated dealer tie-in advertising, and public relations.

Scale. This refers to the absolute size, volume, and impact of the event. These tours run the gamut from smaller individual local events to tours such as the one done by the Harlem Globetrotters, with an audience of more than 1.2 million people.

When considering a sponsorship opportunity and evaluating an event, consider the size and quality of the audience. "Quality" in this case means how closely it matches your own target audience. Promoters sell these tours on numbers and forecasts that are sometimes inaccurate. Event producers will sometimes make shifting and conflicting projections on the number of projected attendees. Push hard on this point. Get it in writing. If possible, get an independent audit of the tour attendees. It is not always possible, but try to scale your contract to the success of the event. For example, you may be able to make a 100 percent payment at a 50,000-attendee level and 40 percent for a 20,000-attendee level.

Paid versus free attendance is another important issue. Some events like Disney PremEars in the Park have free admission. This may affect the demographic profile of the attendees. A free admission also has a big impact of the perceived value of ticket promotions. Others are pay-for-admission events using extensive free-ticket promotion to promote the event through radio stations. While this may help the sponsors gain general awareness of the tour, you should check the percentage of tickets that are sold compared with the share given away. It is usually better to have paid attendees. For a safer bet, look at tours that have been in operation for a number of years with solid operations and logistics.

Once you have a realistic assessment of attendees, you can divide the total cost of the tour by attendance and see how it stacks up compared with other marketing approaches. You must balance the sponsorship with the power of a face-to-face presentation of your brand. The way the tour is executed is part of the scale. Look at the length of the tour, the number and the type of venues. Tours of long duration with many stops can cost a lot in staffing expenses, often more than $200,000.

The type of venue in which the tour appears is also important. When Reebok launched the Reebok Traxtar, they needed an activity area where kids could play, run and jump, and try out the product. Only a larger outside-oriented tour could handle the type of product experience that was necessary to drive the early product adoption. Reebok evaluated the Disney Radio World Tour versus the Disney PremEars in the Park Tour. The radio tour played to indoor theaters and the PremEars played to outside amphitheaters. PremEars won out due to its venue format.

NEGOTIATING THE DEAL

- The contract and the terms of the deal are all very much open for negotiation.

- Watch for hot and marketable events that may sell out fast.
- Ask for an exclusive window on the top sponsorship, thus, locking it up, while you put things in place internally and test the interest with your top retailers.
- Negotiate down the sponsorship cost, or get more for the dollars you spend. We have found the latter strategy most effective.
- Determine your own terms of payment. Most event sponsors ask for all money up front after a letter of intent is signed. Never agree to this. First, legal professionals do not like letters of intent because they are interim documents and by their nature are missing many essential elements. Use a letter of intent as a stepping stone to get to the contract. Agree to pay one-half on contract signing and one-half midway through the tour. Even better, pay in thirds with the last third payable at the successful conclusion of the tour. Build in performance levels with payment (attendees, level of promotion, number of venues, cancellation of the tour, etc.).
- Get all your program ideas and marketing plans built into the contract. Make sure you build in the Internet ideas as part of the contract. Because many entertainment companies hold the Internet as a separate profit center, you may have rights to the tour off-line but not online.
- Watch for conflicting sponsors; get category exclusives. If you use promotional vehicles, make sure you put that in writing. In one tour, a sponsor had Volkswagen "bugs" wrapped to promote its product. At a later point Ford signed with the tour. Ford insisted that no VW bugs be allowed near the tour. A complex negotiation started with all parties. Note that in many cases there are constraints on the venue over which the event management company has no control.
- Leave yourself at least one month for the legal team to work through all the legal issues.

Once all the legal, contact, and payment terms are complete, you need to work closely with the concept creation team and also bring in your own team to make the whole program come together. You really need top staff, who is trained to work with kids and whose background is well checked. So plan to bring in your own staffing. You should audit the early venues and request a report and pictures by e-mail after each venue.

13

DEVELOPING NEW PRODUCTS FOR TWEENS

With the emerging recognition of the tween market a number of companies have begun to develop new products specifically targeting this segment. Based on our work with many leading consumer-products companies, more products will follow. This is not surprising given the dramatic success that some companies have had by being first to offer products that meet the unique needs and wants of tweens. By understanding and then having the courage to develop products for the tween market, several companies have invented what look like entirely new categories, a further testament to the reality and substance of this segment. In this chapter, we will

- review some successful new product entries as a way to highlight what works for this market;
- discuss common mistakes that companies make in developing new products for tweens; and
- offer a roadmap to successful development of new products for tweens.

We will review three cases to gather clues about successful new product development targeting tweens. Our tween all-stars are General Mills' Yoplait Go-Gurt, The Limited's Limited Too, and L'Oréal's L'Oréal Kids. Although they represent three different categories, one common theme unites them all. These companies all focused clearly on understanding the uniqueness of tweens as different from adults, teens, and young kids. In this focus, each company found its own brand of uniqueness and appeal that led to stellar performance.

YOGURT GOES TUBULAR

General Mills has a solid track record of developing successful new products targeting kids and tweens. From Trix cereal to the invention of the fruit snacks category with Fruit Roll-Ups, they have committed themselves to understanding this market and have realized the fruits of their efforts. Their most recent success is in the yogurt category with the introduction of Go-Gurt from Yoplait. Introduced in 1998, Go-Gurt generated $110 million in sales its first year, a big success by most standards.

The key to Go-Gurt's success began with the development of the concept. We can only imagine that this idea must have started out as a technology driven idea—yogurt in a tube. It could have been targeted to anyone. To General Mill's credit, they recognized the potential for this idea to uniquely appeal to kids and tweens. Just think about it—eating yogurt from a tube by squeezing it out into your mouth. Now that's a lot of fun! This is probably the number one rule of new product development for tweens. If it's not fun, forget it.

Rule #1: Make It Fun!

Positioning the product as a "fun way to eat yogurt" taps into the primary driver for almost any tween product concept. Tweens are evolving towards the more serious adolescent years, but they still want to play. This is particularly true of the emerging tween. But, General Mills didn't stop with the form. They made the flavors fun, with tween-appropriate names, such as Berry Blue Blast and Rad Raspberry. They made the package design fun, depicting animated tweens on the go. They also did a great job with our second most important rule of new product development.

Rule #2: It's Just For You

The concept positioning recognizes a tween's world and lifestyle and clearly communicates to the tween that this product is made for you and kids just like you. The name, Go-Gurt, focuses on the idea that this is yogurt you can eat "on the go," and "on the go" is expressed as tween activities—playing sports, skateboarding, and playing music. The characters used on the packaging are obviously tweens, not kids, not teens, and not adults. But, that's not all. Go-Gurt also demonstrates well our third rule of new product development for tweens.

Rule #3: Mom Must Be Appeased

We choose the word "appease" because it is the best way to describe the goal of any successful tween new product concept. It is great if a concept really appeals to moms, but it is critical that they at least are appeased in some way. In the case of Go-Gurt, the concept has just enough wholesomeness to reassure mom that it is yogurt and has good stuff in it, such as fruit. It does not go overboard by communicating all the positive virtues of yogurt—fresh dairy goodness, calcium, and live cultures. This would turn off the tween, and mom already knows this anyway. Remember that it is important to tweens that their moms approve.

LIMITED TOO

They've got 400 stores, they're adding another store every week, and they sell nearly one-half billion dollars worth of silk pajamas, stretch pants, sparkling tops, glitter make-up, and a host of other fashion items that are perfectly tailored to tween girls. It wasn't always this way. Limited Too started out by offering sized-down versions of The Limited's merchandise. However, when CEO Mike Rayden saw the potential and started truly tailoring their merchandise and attitude directly and exclusively to tween girls, things really began to take-off.

This is certainly one of the most successful business ventures that we know of that caters exclusively to tweens. When you look at the delivery of the product concept in the marketplace, it is clear why they are so successful. They rate very strongly on our first three rules of product development and also demonstrate two new rules that further strengthen their proposition.

They've Got Fun

Rule #1. Walk into any Limited Too store and you will see a plethora of clothing styles that are unlike the styles in other stores, such as The Gap or Old Navy. Beyond the basics, their merchandise includes an element of fun that is missing from other stores. Extra-bright colors, glitter and sparkles, even feathers are used to give their clothing a lot more fun and excitement. The stores even have a photo booth to take your picture and then print it out as stickers. They've also got racks of really cool candy right at the cashier station. This is lots more fun than just plain old shopping.

Just for Tween Girls

Rule #2. Everything in the store is just for tween girls. The clothes are just the right sizes. The styles are uniquely tween. Even the music playing in the background is a nonstop playlist of tween girls' favorite artists. The thing adults most notice as different are the ergonomics of the store. The racks are much shorter, but just the right size for the average tween girl who is about 4½ feet tall. The cashier's station is shorter as well, so that the girls do not have to experience the humiliation of walking up to the counter and not being seen. This is their place.

Moms Like It, Too

Rule #3. The management of Limited Too works very hard to not cross the line into styles or items that moms would find offensive. It's a fine line to walk, but they know that it is important to tween girls that their moms approve. After all, mom is still the tween's primary source of funding and, more importantly, her transportation. Look around, and you'll see that virtually all the tween girls are accompanied by their moms. It is clear that the moms are having as much fun as the girls are.

Two New Rules

Limited Too also exemplifies two additional rules of successful concept development for tweens, the first of which is to give the tween more power.

Rule #4: Power is what they're looking for. Tweens are at an age when they are just beginning to spread their wings, and they need reassurance to take the first steps towards independence. This is similar to Rule #2 (It's Just For You), but it goes further to say that you can do this, you can make your own decision, and you will be successful. Limited Too fosters this feeling with everything it does, but the most powerful way is that it gives tween girls respect when they walk into the store. Sales associates are trained to know that the girl is their customer. They talk to the girls, bring them clothes to try on, and treat them like friends. It is heady stuff for a 10-year-old girl to have this much attention paid to her by a cool teenager or young adult.

It is heady stuff for a 10-year-old girl to have this much attention paid to her by a cool teenager or young adult.

No other product or venture we have seen better delivers on our fifth rule of successful concept development than Limited Too. Of course, as a brick-and-mortar retailer, Limited Too has more levers to pull than your average consumer packaged goods marketer. They understand that the tween girl is just becoming aware of the enjoyment of sensory stimulation. Of course, they have the sense of touch in the clothing, but there's lots more they can offer and they do.

Rule #5: There are five senses. Use them. Limited Too designs its in-store merchandising with the feeling of a disco. Bright, pulsating lights and graphics, combined with tween popular music make the store a sight and sound, sensory delight for 8-year-old to 12-year-old girls. With the addition of cosmetics to their line, they also have the advantage of a constant swirl of appealing fragrances. They even have candy to add taste to their sensory offerings. Girls consistently describe Limited Too with the word *overwhelming*, meaning it is exciting to them. By contrast,

Gap Kids, which offers clothing in the same size range, is not nearly as interesting or stimulating to the tween. The lighting is harsh fluorescent-type, and the color scheme is much more monochromatic. No fragrances. No sweet stuff. Definitely more mom-directed. Definitely not as exciting or "overwhelming" for tweens.

L'ORÉAL KIDS CLEANS UP

L'Oréal Kids hair care line is really interesting to us because it brings together all five of our concept development rules and literally stole an entire market segment from under the noses of some powerful consumer packaged goods giants. Johnson & Johnson gave birth to the baby shampoo market. Procter & Gamble cleans up with adults. Neither comprehended the potential of targeting tweens with a unique brand and range of products in the way that L'Oréal did, and, consequently, the other companies are playing catch-up.

Cool Shampoo

L'Oréal Kids is fun (Rule #1). The packaging is brightly colored and vaguely shaped like a fish. It looks weird, but good weird. Tweens tell us all the time that something is weird, and we always ask them if that is a good thing or a bad thing. It's usually a good thing. This is just their way of expressing that something is funny. When L'Oréal first introduced this product line, the entire category was very cosmetic in its look and

feel. They brought to market a tween fashion look that was very clearly aged up from the Johnson & Johnson Baby Shampoo, Winnie-the-Pooh products that were more toy-like and younger in their appeal. L'Oréal did not use any primary colors, which are a clear signal of kid and toddler products. Additionally, they used fun names for the "flavors" of fragrances, such as Burst of Watermelon and Splash of Orange.

What Do You Call a Tween?

L'Oréal Kids is not for moms or babies. It is just for tweens (Rule #2). So, you ask, "Then why didn't they call it L'Oréal Tweens? Doesn't the word 'kids' make it too young?" The answer is maybe, but probably not, given that everything else about the product screams tween. The cool colors and fragrances we mentioned above are too sophisticated for little kids, and tweens know it. We know from our research that tweens do not call themselves tweens—this is a marketing word—and they don't mind being called kids. Marketers who are really trying to differentiate their brands from other younger brands have either avoided using any nomenclature whatsoever or, in the case of Burger King, called them Big Kids. This seems to work, but the most important thing is the *totality* of your concept, not just the target audience designator in the brand name.

Do Tweens Want To Wash Their Hair?

Making products more appealing to tweens is often a big plus for moms (Rule #3), and such is the case for L'Oréal Kids. Some tweens are not yet motivated to take baths or showers, unlike teens whose social sensitivities make them a permanent fixture in the bathroom. Because L'Oréal Kids makes shampooing your hair more exciting for tweens, it is a slam dunk for moms. We can't stress this point enough. Today's moms actually expect and demand products that are designed to appeal to their kids because it makes their jobs easier.

There's Power in the Shower

It's a rite of passage for tweens to begin taking showers and taking care of their hair on their own (Rule #4). L'Oréal Kids offers a whole range of products from shampoos and conditioners in a variety of "flavors" to Tangle Tamer hair spray.

Now tweens have products designed just for them that they can use on their own to take care of their hair. They may not say it out loud, but you just know that tweens are feeling really great, really powerful when they are taking a shower. They're thinking, "This is really cool. I am a big kid now."

Taste the Fragrances

Tweens, and especially girls, love the strong, fruity fragrances that L'Oréal Kids Hair Care products deliver (Rule #5). Because their senses are newly turned on, they revel in L'Oréal's unique yet familiar scents. A few other marketers, Bath and Body Works and Clairol's Herbal Essence, have inadvertently benefited from the tween girl's penchant for powerful fragrances. The fact that most of these fragrances are fruit-based speaks to the idea that you need to lead tweens from the familiar to the novel without relying on them to be too experimental.

So, there you have it—three great brands that have built successful franchises by delighting tweens. They tell us the right way to do it and offer demonstrations of our Five Rules of New Product Development for Tweens. To review, they are as follows:

1. Make it fun.
2. It's just for you.
3. Moms must be appeased.
4. Power is what they are looking for.
5. There are five senses—use them.

OTHER PEOPLE'S MISTAKES OFFER GOOD LESSONS

We can also learn from looking at some of the common mistakes companies make in their new product development efforts to tweens. We know you haven't made any of these mistakes, but we've been around long enough to have seen plenty of misguided efforts. We've even made enough mistakes of our own to know that this is an area of great learning. Of course, the first mistake is to break any of the rules we have already discussed. While some concepts will follow one rule more strongly than another, you will not be successful if you are guilty of actually breaking any one of the five rules. Do not get promoted. Do not collect a bonus. Go directly to another company where you can have a fresh start.

The first and most-often-made mistake actually derives from the culture of many companies. Let's face it, most consumer-products companies have made their fortunes by marketing to mom. Senior managers in most of these companies have no experience in developing or managing products that are marketed directly to kids, tweens, or teens. This leads to the first Big Mistake.

Big Mistake #1: Mom-Centricity

Co-author Tim Coffey tells this story:

Many years ago when I was a young brand manager at Procter & Gamble, I had the truly fortunate assignment to develop new juice products targeting kids. At that time, P&G had no experience in this area, so I was a pioneer in this wilderness of mom-marketed brands. As part of my efforts to teach the company about marketing to kids, I prepared a reel of the then best-in-class TV spots targeting kids for a presentation to senior management. Toy commercials, candy commercials, and cereal commercials were included. They were fun and frenetic and not at all like the slice-of-life commercials for which P&G was famous. I remember to this day the words of John Smale, the Chairman and CEO of P&G at that time, and a man whom I greatly respect and admire. With a look of great consternation, almost bordering on annoyance, and in his deep, resonate voice that would easily pass as the voice of God, he said, "If this is what it takes to market to kids, then we probably shouldn't be in this business."

John Smale knew that the culture of Procter & Gamble was so mom-centric that it would be almost impossible for the company to let go of those instincts so that it could develop truly effective products and develop advertising that targets kids. Unfortunately, in today's world, if you are attempting to develop products for kids, tweens, or teens, you can not let mom-centricity creep into your efforts. Mom-centricity is a heinous disease. It leads either to bad products that likely will not appeal to kids of any age or good products that get killed in the approval process because they do appeal to moms. Mom-centric companies believe appeasing mom (Rule #3) is all you have to do.

There are plenty of examples of successful products that moms really don't like for themselves, but they buy anyway. One such product is Hawaiian Punch Fruit Juicy Blue. No mom on the face of the planet wanted to drink Blue Hawaiian Punch herself. Yet they were appeased by the fact that the product had a full day's supply of vitamin C. Moms bought it because they knew their kids would like it. Too much mom-centricity would have killed this product before it even left the station. There are other examples such as Lunchables Pizza, Trolli Brite Crawlers, and Heinz Green Ketchup. Moms do not like any one of these products, yet each has generated millions of dollars in sales.

At a Kid Power conference we recently attended, someone made the point that a product needs to have an advocate in the home to be successful. So true. We believe, in addition, that if the product is one that is consumed primarily by kids, tweens, or teens, then the advocate had better be the kid, tween, or teen.

The next two big mistakes often made in the development of new products for kids, tweens, or teens are both related to the process of idea generation. The first is a mistake of commission and therefore is forgivable. The second is a mistake of omission and should be severely punished. We have worked with a number of companies who had tried on their own to develop new product concepts for kids, tweens, or teens by conducting brainstorming sessions with the kids. Their intentions were good, but they did not get the results they were looking for.

Big Mistake #2: Making Kids Your Product Developers

Unfortunately, expecting kids, tweens, or teens to come up with winning new product ideas in brainstorming sessions is unrealistic. They are not little brand managers or product developers. They do not have the experience or cognitive capabilities to imagine completely new possibilities. I know this sounds a little like heresy. After all, aren't kids more creative than adults? Well, the answer is, "Not really."

Expecting kids, tweens, or teens to come up with winning new product ideas in brainstorming sessions is unrealistic.

The foundation of creativity is experience. Simply put, with greater experience, there are more new combinations that can be conceived. You must involve kids in the process, but it is not as simple as putting them in a room and asking them to come up with your next big new product. We'll talk later about how to use the insights and inspiration of youth to turbocharge your new product efforts.

So, if you can't just extract great new product ideas from the youths themselves, then maybe great ideas can be created by adults who are in touch with their inner child. In fact, maybe you don't need kids at all. Wrong! This is big mistake #3.

Big Mistake #3: Getting in Touch with Your Inner Child

Companies who think that they can come up with great new product ideas without involving kids, tweens, or teens are really kidding themselves. We've all heard of consultants who come in to help corporate citizens get in touch with their inner child. They will exhort you to be a kid. Now, we're not saying that this is inherently bad. In fact, it is absolutely critical and also a lot of fun, but you cannot stop here. There is no way that we, as adults, can really reproduce from our own childhood what it is like to be a child today. The world is totally different. The experiences and cultural context of today's kids, tweens, and teens are fundamentally unique to them. The charge is not to be a kid, but it is rather to get in touch with kids and loosen up a little.

The last big mistake often committed by companies in their new product efforts is one that was probably created by pressure from retail buyers who value uniqueness in their assortments more than preference by consumers. This leads to the dreaded . . .

Big Mistake #4: Gimmick-itis

In the quest for something that retailers will accept, many youth marketers fall into the trap of Gimmick-itis. It shows itself as gadget-like packaging, the incorrect use of licenses, or as a promotion-based product. Retailers seem to love this kind of stuff, and, therefore, some marketers will give in to this allure. The problem is that it never works for very long. Unless your business plan has the life span of a flea, you will come to regret introducing these types of products. This behavior is particularly prevalent for youth products, based on a misguided notion that because kids really go for this stuff, why bother building a sustainable brand? Gimmick-itis has been rampant in the toy category for a number of years, and the results have been disastrous, with both retailers and manufacturers alike teetering on the brink of bankruptcy.

The undeniable truth is that new products must be based on valid consumer insights and deliver real benefits in new and unique ways. New products based on this foundation have a chance to become brands with tremendous marketplace value. Those that suffer from gimmick-itis will succumb to the disease in short order.

HOW TO FOLLOW THE RULES AND AVOID THE BIG MISTAKES

At WonderGroup, we have developed a comprehensive approach to new product development for kids, tweens, and teens (we'll refer to them all now as kids) that is based on following the rules and avoiding the big mistakes. Of course, we also have a secret ingredient that we call "wonder." This is what clients such as General Mills, Heinz, Kodak, Quaker Oats, Johnson & Johnson, Warner-Lambert, and many others pay us for. It is the uncanny ability to see the invisible. It is the sensitivity to true insights. It is also the undying love of kids that makes us really good at what we do. Having made that less-than-humble point, we will now share our secrets.

Following are the four major components to our product development process:

1. Insight
2. Inspiration
3. Invention
4. Intelligence

Insight

We have learned that new product development efforts are significantly more productive if they are based on insights. We've discussed elsewhere in this book the techniques that can be used to derive insights, so we won't repeat them here. The key is to focus creative energies into specific areas that have been determined to represent high potential. For example, we learned in one candy project that tweens really liked to interact with their candy, so we focused much of our creative energies on the development of new ideas that involved some sort of interactivity. In another project, we identified that enhancing social interaction was a key insight in the product category we were working in. Therefore, our creative efforts could focus on this area of high potential and avoid wasting time and energy in other less fruitful directions.

Making some decisions about where to focus is essentially the development of a strategy for the project. It is typical that we will end up focusing on as many as three different areas. By highlighting each one, we are assured of giving enough attention to it, while avoiding the pitfall of having ideas only in one area. We find that this approach produces more balance as well as higher-quality ideas.

Inspiration

As we have already discussed, it is critical to involve the kids in the process of developing new products, but you cannot rely on them to come up with fully formed concepts. What they can do is inspire breakthrough ideas. We design "ideation" events to specifically meet project objectives. These events, however, are comprised of the following three basic components:

1. Creative Animals
2. Homework
3. BrainGaming

First and most important are the kids themselves. We do not want representative or average kids for the inspiration phase of our process. This is not research, where we want a representative sample. We need kids who are exceptionally creative, bright, and comfortable working with both peers and adults. We find these kids by using special screening questions and by tapping such organizations as Odyssey of the Mind, a national creativity program and competition for youths. These special kids, who love to create, are a joy to work with. We call them "Creative Animals."

In general, this work must be done with tweens and teens, as kids under age 8 are not usually articulate or cognitively developed enough to brainstorm productively. For projects targeting this younger group we will use 8 to 9 year olds and moms. Further, the insight phase of the project for younger children becomes even more important. In addition to kids and moms, we may use creative experts, such as teachers, art instructors, toy developers, and so forth, to provide an extra dimension of inspiration to the process.

The next component is "Homework," a homework assignment for the kids that is custom designed to fit the project at hand. The kids receive their assignment about one week prior to the event. Typically, we ask them to do something that immerses them in the category in which we are interested. For example, for a candy project, we sent the kids five of the top ten candy bars. Their assignment was to eat the candy bars and write their reactions in a journal. Tough work, isn't it? We also asked them, as the price of admission to the event, to bring at least ten new ideas that were consistent with our objectives. The real point of all this is to "pre-seed" their minds with thoughts and experiences about the category or topic. Remember, kids do not yet have the wealth of experience that adults do, so we give them a targeted remedial course. They come to our event prepared to be creative.

The next and central component of our inspiration event is "Brain-Gaming." We call our ideation process BrainGaming because we design the experience to be like play. This is more compatible with the youth psyche and cognitive development. It is unlike traditional brainstorming that is primarily a verbal effort. By playing BrainGames with the kids, we get around any limitations in their verbal abilities or any self-consciousness that might limit their thinking. One game we play almost always when developing food products is Hands On. In this exercise, we let the kids create their own new product idea from hundreds of ingredients. We find it informative to observe the kinds of combinations the kids put together and to hear how they describe those combinations. We have many different types of games that we will use to fit the specific project we are working on, as well as the particular age group. They all accomplish one goal—to keep the kids in a fun and energized state of creativity.

Coming out of an inspiration event, we will have thousands of ideas and fragments of ideas. We call them "sparks." Now comes the magic.

Invention

This is hard work. Our team of experienced product developers and creatives takes the sparks and begins to develop rough concepts. We use the sparks as stimuli to generate the ideas, cycling through phases of generation, sifting the best ideas, and then building on these. This is intense work that requires absolute concentration. We always do this outside of the office to avoid being distracted. We write the ideas on a form (see Figure 13.1). Then we think through each idea in terms of the key insight from which it is derived, the emotional benefit, the functional benefit, a physical description of the product, and ideas for keeping the idea fresh over time.

FIGURE 13.1

Invention Diagram

How, when, and where would you use this product?

What are the main reasons for using your new product?

How will your new product make me feel?

What will keep me coming back for more?

© Copyright 1999 WonderGroup Inc.

The next phase of our invention process is what we call "Darwiniza-tion." It is a creative and decision-making routine that involves the client team. From a big-picture standpoint, this is where the client team works with us through the following series of steps:

1. Selection
2. Mutation
3. Extinction

We bring to this phase a large number of high-potential concepts that are based on the inspiration of the kids. At this point, we work through the concepts with a broader team of people who will bring even more creativity to the ideas. We suggest to our clients that they include people from marketing, research and development, marketing research, sales and manufacturing, and any other departments they feel should have ownership in the final ideas. We have found that it is best not to include senior managers in this phase because they usually are not used to being in a creative mode and can stifle other members of the team. Of course, there are exceptions to this rule.

We guide the team through selecting the obvious strong ideas and then set those aside for the moment. We then take the remaining ideas and have subteams of the group work with these ideas to mutate some of them into stronger ideas. Next, we do the same with the initially selected ideas. Finally, we make decisions as a team regarding the concepts that will move forward. The ideas not chosen are extinct. We now have a predetermined number of concepts that the whole team agrees are ready to move to the next step.

Intelligence

With our final ideas in hand, we can develop fully illustrated concept boards to show to kids for their reactions. We always do a quick, but critical, qualitative check of the concepts before quantitative testing just to be sure we haven't missed something. Kids are brutal on details, so you do not want to kill an idea because you missed something stupid. We are reminded of an example of a microwave food concept where we illustrated that the final product was hot by showing little squiggly lines of steam rising up from the food. Makes sense, right? When we showed this to kids, however, they hated the concept because they thought it would stink! We were puzzled to say the least, and we asked, "Why would you say that this food would stink?" They said, "You can see the smell rising up from the food. It must really stink!"

After checking the details, we go to quantitative testing with the confidence that the idea will live or die on its own merits. Some clients have asked us whether it is necessary to quantitatively test the concepts that we develop, and our answer is always yes. A number of good concept screening research companies will provide excellent guidance regarding the sales potential of new product concepts. We are very good, but we are not infallible. Because taking new product concepts to the next stage of prototype development is expensive and time-consuming, it would not be intelligent to move ahead without sound research.

CONCLUSION

This chapter has provided you with some practical guidance on new product development for tweens that will increase your odds of success in the marketplace. There are many opportunities for marketers to create big and profitable businesses by targeting tweens, as long as you follow a systematic process.

14

RESEARCHING AND STAYING IN TOUCH

We have talked before about the need for today's marketers to get kids to stay in touch with the rapidly changing kids marketplace. Fortunately, there are many ways to do this.

EXISTING RESEARCH AND ONGOING STUDIES

Just about all of the major kids media companies conduct and willingly share research on the kids segment with potential media buyers. *Disney Adventures, Sports Illustrated for Kids,* Nickelodeon, Cartoon Network, MTV, and Next Generation Radio are among the many media sources available for data.

Syndicated studies such as the Roper Youth Report, Yankelovich Youth MONITOR, TRU Teen Study, and the Simmons Kid Study are also available for those companies willing to pay for information.

PRIMARY RESEARCH

Talking to and hearing directly from kids is still the best thing you can do when it comes to capturing important information. Focus groups, online panels, and one-on-one interviews all play meaningful roles here.

One of the most-used methods for staying in touch with tweens and obtaining their opinions is focus groups. When conducting focus groups with tweens, Ruth Jackson, kids moderator for C&R Research advises:

> Keep in mind that tweens are truly between earlier childhood (family-based, limited influences and horizons) and the teen years still to come (peer focused, rebellious, and ever-expanding horizons and experiences). Successful qualitative tween research combines designs and techniques that make the best of both of these aspects of the tween world.

Successful qualitative research makes the most of the "younger side" of tweens—their openness and willingness to share their private side—heartfelt personal opinions and emotions—all expressed without strong peer influence. At the same time, it can leverage the potential benefits to be discovered in the "older side" of tweens—their developed conceptual thinking and increased ability in expressing their ideas and opinions. Also, as "older kids" they are rapidly expanding their life experiences (independent of family) and are beginning to develop true personal preferences based on individual tastes and interests.

Boys and girls should be separated because the majority of their interests and preferences are very gender specific.

When conducting focus group research among tweens, we have found that it is best to attempt to keep the ages in each group to a two-year level or two-grade-level age span. Three years of development is just too broad an age difference for kids under age 12 or 13 to be experiencing the same reactions to most products. If possible, boys and girls should be separated because the majority of their interests and preferences are very gender specific, and we oftentimes witness at least some posturing between the sexes. Other tips for interviewing tweens versus other ages are shown in Figure 14.1.

Here is one caution: While focus groups continue to be an excellent way in which to generate hypotheses and "hear" tweens talk about subjects in their own words, we strongly caution companies not to act solely on the basis of focus groups alone. While this seems obvious, we can't tell you how many major companies we see make multimillion dollar decisions based solely on their interpretations of a dozen or so people in focus groups. While this is a caution for focus groups of any kind, it is especially important advice to heed when working with kids and tweens.

We continually find that tweens can be "master" actors in focus groups. They are, after all, very aware of and concerned with rules, fitting in, and

FIGURE 14.1

Qualitative Research Tips

	KIDS 4 TO 7	TWEENS 8 TO 12	TEENS 13 TO 18
Size	Friendship pairs/ small groups (3 to 5 kids)	Can be larger (6 to 8 kids)	Full size (8 to 10) or friendship pairs if topic more personal
Gender	Single gender	Single gender	Can be mixed
Length	Short (20 to 60 minutes)	Longer (90 to 120 minutes)	Can be 2 hours
Warmup	Longer to establish comfort level	May be decreased, have greater social skills	Longer, greater need to establish trust
Activities	Easy, varied, physical	More complex, physical	Can be cerebral
Stimuli	Stimulus-oriented concepts vs. conceptual	Conceptual ideas okay, but additional stimulus to reinforce concepts better	Can be very conceptual
Rating	Can tell likes/dislikes but have difficulty rating	Can effectively compare and evaluate differences using scales	More advances analytical skills
Exercises	Gather individual opinions, avoid teamwork	Good team players, teamwork bonds group	Prefer individual self expression, more independence
Setting	Kid-friendly, kid-sized furniture	Casual, but not set up for young children	Casual, but not set up for young children
Prework	All pregroup homework should be filtered through parent	Most want to do their own assignments, can take responsibility	Most want to do their own assignments, can take responsibility

above all peer acceptance. Each of these concerns can cause them to be influenced by others in the focus group. In fact, virtually every time that we have personally interviewed tweens in a one-on-one situation, their opinions and answers seem to change significantly compared with what we heard them express in groups. To supplement information on tweens, sometimes it is rewarding to interview their parents and especially to talk to teachers, coaches, and other influential adults. Unlike the situation with teens, parents, teachers, and coaches often have a good feel for what is going on in tween lives and can provide valuable research input. Teens, on the other hand, confide primarily in their friends. As mothers of teens will sadly tell you, their teen daughters just don't confide in them anymore.

We continually find that tweens can be "master" actors in focus groups.

When looking for more accurate understandings and measurements of tween opinions, you must rely on quantitative techniques. One-on-one interviews, conducted in various cities, by mall intercept is probably the most traditional way to accomplish this. Phone interviews and parent-assisted mail interviews are also sometimes useful. At the very least, we recommend that you conduct at least some one-on-one interviews, even if they are in one city and even if it is just among a few dozen tweens. This is one of the best ways in which to be certain that you minimize potential group and peer pressure bias.

Many research companies offer quantitative testing services, but make certain that whoever you choose has extensive experience in interviewing and collecting data from kids. Many rely on having moms ask the questions. Watch out for possible biases here, too. Just as there are important tips to know about qualitative research, quantitative research should also be done by people with experience with various kid ages.

Thanks to the huge number of tweens now on the Internet, the newest method available for securing fast, quantifiable data is to use kids online test panels. These panels allow marketers to have efficient access to thousands of kids across the country and can provide answers to questions within a few days of fielding. Established research organizations that offer these panels include NFO, Harris Interactive Panel, and KidzEyes.com.

Because online panels allow kids to answer questions themselves in a totally involving, nonthreatening manner, free from group bias, answers derived with this method could prove quite valuable. As of 2003, the vast majority of U.S. tweens will have access to the Internet making these panels even more representative of the general tween population. A study by CPB estimated Internet access at home to be as high as 78 percent. However, use caution when trying to assess information that might be more relevant to certain tween segments, such as low income kids, because some groups are still underrepresented online.

Screening

Many of today's marketers have found quantitative research to be particularly helpful for screening preliminary new product and ad concepts. This type of research allows marketers to expose a number of different concepts to a relatively large number of tweens (and sometimes their moms) in order to help determine which concepts have the best likelihood for success.

Quantitative research can prove invaluable to any company looking to launch new items to today's tweens. It can help marketers determine the strongest ideas from among a list of many potential opportunities. It can also save companies significant expense by helping them avoid the mistake of developing products whose basic premise might be too weak to succeed. Quantitative research can also prove helpful in understanding whether it is the tween or the parent who is the best target for the concept as well as helping you fine-tune the positioning of the final idea.

One such testing organization, AcuPoll, allows marketers to screen from one to many concepts among a group of about 50 tweens to 100 tweens and a separate group of their moms. Testing is conducted in a central location, and each concept is rated for characteristics such as uniqueness, perceived taste (if a food), and overall likelihood to purchase, among other characteristics. Ratings from tweens and parents help marketers determine the overall strength of the idea and whether the strength is best represented among tweens, their parents, or both groups. Also, you can assess whether parents might be too much of a barrier in the case of some new concepts—possibly signaling a major problem no matter how much tweens like the product in question.

Overall results are compared with norms derived from the previous testing of thousands of other concepts, and marketers have a better idea as to the likelihood their concept will succeed. Then they are in better position to determine whether it is worth investing significantly more funds into product development and support.

Modeling

Some traditional consumer package goods companies elect not to even test market a new product until they have received volume estimates from an established modeling group like Bases, FYI, and others. Unfortunately, most traditional modeling formulas do not know how to take into account the importance of kid influence, kid-focused media, and promotions in forecasting the overall sales volume of a kid-oriented item. As a result, forecasts may be unrealistically low.

If you are going to use modeling services, here too make certain that they have a thorough understanding of the true dynamics of purchasing that takes place for tween-consumed products.

IMPLICATIONS

- No matter what strategy you might be considering, take the time to secure the opinions of your tween target audience before actually implementing the effort.
- While focus groups are a typical method used to secure tween opinions and attitudes, they must be used solely for hypothesis generation.
- When conducting focus groups with tweens, be especially careful of the potential likelihood of group bias and peer pressure affecting tween comments.
- Always use individual one-on-one interviews, surveys, or other quantitative test methods to confirm the hypotheses drawn from focus groups.
- When developing new tween products, consider the potential time and cost savings offered through concept screening research.
- Whenever using any research company, make certain that it has ample experience in kid marketing.

2003 Yankelovich Youth MONITOR. Chapel Hill: Yankelovich, 2003.

Acuff, Dan. S. and Robert H. Reiher. *What Kids Buy and Why: The Psychology of Marketing to Kids.* New York: The Free Press, 1997.

"Advertising to Kids Creative." *KidScreen.* February 2000.

Ahuja, Roshan D., Louis Capella, Ronald Taylor. "Child Influences, Attitudinal and Behavioral Comparisons between single parent and dual parent households in grocery shopping decisions," *Journal of Marketing Theory and Practice.* Vol. 6, No. 1, (Winter 1998).

Arnold, Morgan J., PhD. *NeoPets 2002 Study: The Wireless Generation.* March 25 2002.

Berk, Laura E. *Child Development.* New York: Allyn & Bacon, 1989.

Children, Families, and the Internet. San Mateo: Grunwald Associates, 2003.

Day, M.C. *Advances in Child Development and Behavior.* New York: H.W. Reese, 1975.

Del Vecchio, Eugene. *Creating Ever-Cool, A Marketer's Guide to a Kid's Heart.* Greta, LA: Pelican Publishing Company, 1998.

Expenditures on Children by Families, Annual Report 2002. USDA Center for Nutrition Policy and Promotion. Miscellaneous Publication Number: 1528-2002.

Exploring the Digital Generation Conference. Washington, D.C. September 22–23, 2003.

Fields, Jason. "Children's Living Arrangements and Characteristics: March 2002." *Current Population Reports: Population Characteristics.* Issued June 2003.

Girls Speak Out: Teens Before Their Time @ 2000. Girl Scouts of the United States of America, 2000.

Goldsmith, Diane. "Is room décor the next hot thing for teens and tweens?" *Philadelphia Inquirer.* May 9, 2003.

Grieco, Elizabeth and Rachel Cassidy. "Overview of Race and Hispanic Origin 2000." *Census 2000 Brief.* Issued March 2001.

Harris Interactive Youth Pulse. Rochester: Harris Interactive, 2003.

"How Kids and Tweens Use and Respond to Radio." Arbitron Kids/Tweens Ratings and Callbacks Study. Winter 2000.

"Kids take on high-end fashion," *Women's Wear Daily.* May 30, 2000.

Konsius, Jura. "Targeting Tweens: Marketers finding room to grow," *The Washington Post.* March 28, 2000.

LaFerla, Ruth. "Teenage Shoppers (Purses to Brinks)." *The New York Times.* September 11 and 20, 2000.

McNeal, James U. *Kids Market: Myths and Realities.* Ithaca, NY: Paramount Market Publishing, Inc., 1999.

National Center for Education Statistics. http://nces.ed.gov/fastfacts/.

Neuborne, Ellen and Kathleen Kerwin. "Generation Y: Today's teens—the biggest bulge since the boomers—may force marketers to toss their old tricks." *Business Week.* February 15, 1999.

Nick.com/Nielsen/NetRatings Spring 2003 Data. http://www.nielsen-netratings.com.

Roberts, Donald F., Ulla G. Foehr, Victoria J. Rideout, and Mollyann Brodie. *Kids & Media: The New Millennium, Los Angeles, CA: A Kaiser Family Foundation Report.* November 1999.

Roper Youth Report. New York: Roper Starch Worldwide, 2003.

Rosen, Elliott. *Anatomy of a Buzz: How to Create Word-of-Mouth Marketing.* New York, Doubleday, 2000.

Simmons, Tavia and Martin O'Connell. Married-Couple and Unmarried-Partner Households: 2000. *Census 2000 Special Reports.* Issued February 2003.

Simmons Market Research Bureau, Kids Fall and Spring 2002 Data.

Smith, J. Walker and Ann Clurman. *Rocking the Ages: The Yankelovich Report on Generational Marketing.* New York: Harper Business, 1997.

Sports Illustrated for Kids Omnibus Studies. New York: Sports Illustrated for Kids, February–May 1993 and February–May 2000.

Thompson, Michael. *Speaking of Boys: Answers to the Most-Asked Questions about Raising Boys.* New York: Ballantine Books, 2000.

The Kids and Tweens Listening Study, 2000. Arbitron, 2000 (http://www.arbitron.com)

Van Evra, Judith Page. *Television and Child Development.* New York: Lawrence Erlbaum Associates Inc., 1997.

Wurzel, Barbara J. "Growing Up in Single Parent Families." Single Parent Central: On-Line Resources for Single Parent Families (http://www.singleparentcentral.com).

Zollo, Peter. *Wise Up to Teens: Insights into Marketing and Advertising to Teenagers.* Ithaca: New Strategist Publications, 1999.

DAVID L. SIEGEL

Dave has been marketing to kids for more than 20 years. After several years of classic consumer packaged goods marketing for such companies as Procter & Gamble, Bristol Myers Drackett, and others, Dave moved over to the advertising and consulting field where he became enamored with the kids marketplace.

As one of the first classic consumer marketers to realize the potential of marketing to kids, Dave has had the opportunity of helping dozens of companies in just about every industry realize and capitalize on the potential of marketing to kids. Among his many clients have been companies such as Hasbro, Warner-Lambert, Motorola, JVC, Smucker's, Borden, Chiquita, Curad, Toymax, Chupa Chups, and Trolli.

Over the years, Dave has addressed such groups as the U.S. Olympic Committee, Grocery Manufacturer's Association, Color Marketing Group, School Home & Office Association, as well as several AMA chapters and the Retail Merchandising Conference regarding kids marketing. He has chaired or spoken at virtually every kids marketing conference in the country and is also on the advisory board for KidPower and Selling to Kids.

In 1998, Dave joined forces with Tim Coffey and Greg Livingston and became president of WonderGroup, now one of the leading youth marketing and advertising firms in the United States.

Dave, his wife Jan, and their children Robin, Adam, Lauren, and Tiffany live in Cincinnati.

TIMOTHY J. COFFEY

As co-founder and Chairman/CEO of WonderGroup, Tim has led the company to become a leader in youth marketing, with such prestigious clients as ConAgra, General Mills, Hasbro, Heinz, Johnson & Johnson, Kellogg, Kodak, Nickelodeon, PepsiCo, and Proctor & Gamble, among others.

Tim has been an avid student of consumer behavior for over 20 years, beginning with his tenure at Procter & Gamble where he worked as a consumer researcher, new product innovator, and brand manager across a variety of categories. Tim joined Tupperware as Director of Marketing and New Products, where he led that company to its first growth in a decade, reinventing and successfully extending the brand to meet the needs of today's young families. His passion for kids marketing was ignited while at Procter & Gamble, when Tim had the good fortune to manage and relaunch both the Sunny Delight and Hawaiian Punch brands. Tim helped bring the classic "Punchy" character back to kids after a 15-year hiatus, and he invented miniature-size Sunny Delight bottles that helped put this brand in kids' lunch boxes everywhere.

His daily passion, however, comes from his own "living focus group" of four daughters—Sara, 17; Kathleen, 14; Shannon, 11; Elizabeth, 7—and wife Jill.

GREGORY LIVINGSTON

Greg got his first taste of advertising to youth and family in 1982 at the Direct Marketing Group in New York where he was assigned to the Nestlé and Sitmar Cruise accounts. After later stints at Rapp Collins, the direct marketing arm of Doyle Dane Bernbach, and Stockton West Burkhart in Cincinnati, Greg jumped to the client side, spending 10 years as vice president of marketing and advertising for LCA-Vision. LCA-Vision, a medical services organization, evolved into the nation's largest network of laser centers for correction of myopia (a procedure now called LASIK).

After LCA-Vision went public in 1996, Greg got the itch to get back into the agency business and joined Sive/Young & Rubicam, where he had the fortunate opportunity to be only two offices away from Dave Siegel. Greg immediately became enamored of youth marketing as Dave espoused the principles and fascinating nuances of how to communicate to younger generations.

Leaving with Dave in 1998 to join Tim Coffey in the formation of WonderGroup, Greg has been involved in youth-focused product development and advertising for many companies, including Chiquita, General Mills, ConAgra, Nickelodeon, Lipton, Hasbro, Kellogg's, Heinz, Ore-Ida, Kodak, Johnson & Johnson, Totes/Isotoner, and Proctor & Gamble. Greg, along with Tim and Dave, has chaired and/or presented topical subjects at youth conferences and corporations across the country.

Greg and his wife Paula, a clinical social worker who specializes in adolescents, have three boys, Ryan, 11; Graham, 9; and Ian, 2.

WONDERGROUP

WonderGroup is the nation's leading independent youth and young family marketing and communications agency. Tim, Dave, and Greg lead client initiatives that range from research and product development to promotion and advertising campaigns. The company uses its extensive knowledge of moms and their kids to understand consumer needs, and then creates marketing solutions that help companies dramatically grow sales and profits.

WonderGroup provides insights and communications that are built around the three strategic imperatives critical to getting and keeping today's moms and their kids (kids, tweens, and teens) involved with client brands: Recognition, Reward, and Relationship. The unique strength of WonderGroup is its integrated approach. The agency brings research and branding, strategic development of marketing and communication programs, and the implementation of these programs together to target focused, geo-demographic segments of kids, tweens, teens and young families (moms). Tim, Dave, and Greg manage a staff of over 40 professionals dedicated to providing expert marketing services.

For additional information about WonderGroup, please visit http://www.wondergroup.com or call any of the authors at 513-357-2950.

Share the message!

Bulk discounts
Discounts start at only 10 copies. Save up to 55% off retail price.

Custom publishing
Private label a cover with your organization's name and logo. Or, tailor information to your needs with a custom pamphlet that highlights specific chapters.

Ancillaries
Workshop outlines, videos, and other products are available on select titles.

Dynamic speakers
Engaging authors are available to share their expertise and insight at your event.

**Call Dearborn Trade Special Sales at 1-800-245-BOOK (2665)
or e-mail trade@dearborn.com**

Dearborn™
Trade Publishing
A **Kaplan Professional** Company